A GUIDE TO CHAUCER'S METER

ARTHUR WAYNE GLOWKA
Georgia College

UNIVERSITY
PRESS OF
AMERICA

Lanham • New York • London

Copyright © 1991 by

University Press of America®, Inc.

4720 Boston Way
Lanham, Maryland 20706

3 Henrietta Street
London WC2E 8LU England

Library of Congress Cataloging-in-Publication Data

Glowka, Arthur Wayne.
A guide to Chaucer's meter / Arthur Wayne Glowka.
p.   cm.
Includes bibliographical references.
1. Chaucer, Geoffrey, d. 1400—Versification.   2. English
language—Middle English, 1100-1500—Versification.   I. Title.
PR1951.G57   1991
821'.1—dc20   90–23781 CIP

ISBN 0–8191–8145–5 (cloth)
ISBN 0–8191–8146–3 (pbk.)

OCLC: 2276 4877

 The paper used in this publication meets the minimum requirements of
American National Standard for Information Sciences—Permanence
of Paper for Printed Library Materials, ANSI Z39.48–1984.

TABLE OF CONTENTS

Preface   *v*

One: Some Basics   1

Two: Rhythm and Meter in Modern English   17

Three: Chaucer's Regular Iambic Pentameter Lines   31

Four: The Syllables That Count   41

Five: Some Basic Substitutions   53

Six: Chaucer's Four-Stress Meter   65

Seven: The Metrical Abstraction and the Rhythmic Realization   79

Additional Suggested Reading   93

Preface

This book gives step-by-step lessons in the scansion of Chaucer's verse. It offers arguments in favor of foot-scansion and is therefore traditional in its treatment of the subject. Although the method of scansion is traditional, the presentation of the method does not become insistent on narrow readings. Indeed, the final chapter of the book discusses the rhythm of Chaucer's verse and points out the usefulness of rhythmic scansion.

The first chapters lead the reader into Chaucer's versification through the study of Modern English stress and meter. With this type of introduction, the reader unfamiliar with prosody can gain a basic understanding of the general subject as it applies to Modern English—a familiar language—before grappling with Chaucer's Middle English. The later chapters take up Chaucer's "regular" lines of iambic pentameter, the problem of the final unaccented *e*, metrical substitutions, and Chaucer's four-stress meter. Throughout, the discussion makes allowances for alternative ways of solving problems. Each chapter provides exercises that allow the reader to practice with examples of the material under question.

The book is envisioned as a supplemental text for use in courses on Chaucer or English prosody, but a bright student could read the book on his or her own to learn about Chaucer's meter. Although book-length traditional treatments of Chaucer's versification are available in academic libraries, these books are in many ways outdated and have suffered from years of attacks by strident critics. This book dusts off the traditional account of Chaucer's verse and presents it within the context of modern polemics about meter. With its introductory explanation of the concepts of meter, the book fills a particular gap in the literature about Chaucer's meter and will be especially helpful for modern students (and teachers), who often lack formal training in English versification.

I present this book with the firm belief that the greatest delights of Chaucer's poetry cannot be translated. The music, if you will, of his verse is distinct and is lost to modern ears without some training and hard work. Despite some inherent difficulties, it is possible to gain a clear understanding of the metrical patterns of Chaucer's poetry. If this book contributes in any way to that understanding, it will be serving its purpose.

Acknowledgements

This book would not have been possible without the help and support of many colleagues, teachers, and friends. This project would still be an unrealized idea if it were not for grants from the Georgia College Faculty Development and Faculty Research Committees for supplies, interlibrary loan fees, travel, and release time. Special thanks are due to Robert Bartos for his initial advocacy of the project and to Marjorie Prentice and Thomas F. Armstrong for their friendly accommodation of a project with many stops and starts. Untold hours were devoted to this project by Nancy Dyer, who administered the interlibrary loan services of the Ina Dillard Russell Library at Georgia College with profound efficiency. Too much, perhaps, of this book is built from the ideas of others, and I owe much to my teachers of Chaucer and English prosody. To my father, Arthur John Glowka, I give thanks for unwittingly teaching me the opening lines of *The General Prologue* in the text of a Dale Carnegie speech. To my ninth-grade English teacher, Dorothy Everett, I give thanks for a clear-headed explanation of iambic pentameter. To my first formal Chaucer teacher, James H. Sledd, I give thanks for the fear that made me study Chaucer and Chaucer's meter harder than anything I had ever studied before. To Thomas Cable, I give thanks for the best training in prosody I believe one can get. And to W. Bruce Finnie and Mark Amsler, I give thanks for teaching me how to explain meter to others. In addition, I thank my chairman, R. B. Jenkins, for his enthusiastic encouragement, even when enthusiasm was not deserved. Special thanks are due to Barbara Lahey for help with preparing camera-ready copy, and we both thank Ron Trice and Barbara Brannon, our Macintosh gurus. Finally, I thank my wife, Ellen, for proofreading and for having sense enough to avoid letting a project like this interrupt the intimacy of our lives.

One: Some Basics

As a student of Chaucer, you no doubt know that Chaucer wrote and spoke in English, but that the English he knew was very different from the English we now speak and write. Unfortunately, we will never be able to hear Chaucer read his verse. The actual sound of Chaucer's voice is lost forever, and we have no hope of coming upon a true House of Fame where all utterances resound forever. However, we can make fairly reliable guesses about the sounds of Chaucer's English. Over the last couple of centuries scholars have been studying Chaucer's English, and although we will never know for sure how Chaucer spoke, we can establish some basic guidelines about how we think he might have spoken. These details are covered in histories of the English language, in handbooks on Middle English, and in guides to Chaucer's language. These works may differ in detail, but in general they present the same view: Chaucer pronounced all the consonants he wrote and sounded his vowels with more or less continental values. With a few notable and predictable exceptions, he also accented his words much like we do.

This last detail is very important, for accent is the main concern of this book. Accent, or stress, is the most important organizer of poetic form in English and has been so throughout the history of English poetry. Although some people do not have much of an ear for stress, most people can learn to distinguish different levels of stress. Most people, therefore, with a little work can learn how to scan poetry, that is, to figure out its organizing form.

Stress is the means by which speakers of many dialects of Modern English distinguish between the following words:

> *permit*, a noun as in "I have a hunting *permit*."
> *permit*, a verb as in "I cannot *permit* you to do that."

One way to signal that one syllable of a word has stronger stress than another syllable is to place an accent over the stronger syllable. According to this scheme, we would distinguish the forms of *permit* like this:

/
permit *(noun)*

/
permit *(verb)*

There are other pairs of words that we can distinguish by the same scheme:

/   /
abstract *(noun)* / abstract *(verb)*

/   /
contract *(noun)* / contract *(verb)*

In these examples, however, more than stress is at work. When the different forms are pronounced, the vowels are also different. The noun form of *abstract*, for example, has a low front vowel in the stressed syllable; the verb form has the reduced vowel schwa in the same syllable.

In the case of *permit*, stress is *phonemic*. This means that stress is used to distinguish between two essentially different words. However, stress is not always phonemic. In isolation, a word of one syllable gets stress:

/   /
black   her

In words of more than one syllable, the stress on a syllable may be determined by the form of the word or the historical source of a word. With a considerable amount of study, a student could come to some understanding about how the history of the English language determines the stress assignments of English words, but in general, native speakers know by and large how to stress English words without recourse to etymology or complicated rules. When in doubt about a stress placement, an English speaker may refer to a standard dictionary where he will find the generally accepted pronunciation of a word, and for most people this kind of reference is sufficient. However, since some people have trouble hearing and analyzing stress placements, it is a good idea for us to look at a few words.

Grammatical categories and word history provide the criteria for determining stress placements. Words of two syllables are generally stressed on the first syllable:

```
    /       /       /       /
 father  redder  noble  twosome

    /       /       /       /
 fishing  fiction  able  Shakespeare
```

When a two-syllable word has been recently borrowed from a foreign language, it may retain the accent of the original language:

```
    /          /        /
 cliche   noblesse  oblige
```

A similar pattern can be seen in native verbs and prepositions based on compounds:

```
    /          /
 become     upset

    /          /
 between    without
```

The pattern also appears in borrowed verbs that have been otherwise Anglicized or made to sound English:

```
    /          /        /
 complete   repel   distill
```

Although accounting for the knowledge about stress that English speakers have is fraught with complexity, we can be thankful both as speakers of English and students of English poetry that we already know a great deal about the sounds of English words. To see that we are all basically in agreement, I offer the list of words below for practice.

Exercise 1.1

Directions: Identify the stressed syllable in each word.

houses
ringer
brother
little

compute
belief
object *(noun)*
object *(verb)*
fishing
critic
essay
handle
diction
comma
commit
comet
awful
fulfill

Words of more than two syllables require us to refine our notion of stress. Take for example the following words:

elevator

dictionary

operator

Elizabethan

In each of these words we clearly have one syllable that is more strongly stressed than all of the others:

/   /
elevator   dictionary

/   /
operator   Elizabethan

But in each of these words there is also another syllable that seems to have some prominence as a stressed syllable. This syllable seems to be weaker than the main-stressed syllable but stronger than the other syllables. We can introduce a new symbol to signify this stress:

```
 /  \    /   \
elevator  dictionary

 /  \     \  /
operator  Elizabethan
```

We call the level of stress signified by the forward slash *primary stress*. The backward slash is used to signify *tertiary stress* (the term *secondary stress* is reserved for a different kind of stress). To see once again that we are all hearing the same things, try the following exercise.

Exercise 1.2
Directions: Identify the primary and tertiary stresses in the words below:

destitution
commissary
compensation
testimony
complication
emaciation
secretary
computation
introduction

You may remember that when we started, we said that words in isolation generally have stress. In our new terms, we can say that these words have primary stress. However, when these isolated words are put next to others in some kind of context, some of the words undergo a change. In many contexts, for example, nouns and adjectives retain primary stress. However, when nouns and adjectives are thrown together in an immediate context, one of them is demoted; that is, it loses its primary stress. We then can say that the noun or adjective has secondary stress where it once had primary stress. We can account for secondary stress with two rules: the *Compound Stress Rule* and the *Nuclear Stress Rule* (Halle and Keyser 15-31).

The compound stress rule can be applied when a compound word is formed from two other words:

stone + wall = stonewall (*verb or nickname*)

In isolation, both stone and wall have primary stress. When they are combined into one word, the stress of the second element is demoted. It is often said that the Compound Stress Rule throws the stress to the left. The first element thus retains the primary stress and the second element loses it:

```
   /      /      /    ^
stone  +  wall  =  stonewall
```

The caret (^) symbolizes secondary stress. Here are some more examples:

```
   /      /      /    ^
black + bird  =  blackbird
```

```
   /      /      /    ^
book +  keeper = bookkeeper
```

```
   /      /      /    ^
light + house  = lighthouse
```

Exercise 1.3
Directions: Assign stress to the words in the following formulas:

blue + jay = bluejay
mocking + bird = mockingbird
house + keeping = housekeeping
class + room = classroom
car + pool = carpool

The Nuclear Stress Rule, on the other hand, is commonly said to throw stress to the right. The Nuclear Stress Rule governs the assignment of stress in phrases. The main syllable of the main word of the phrase gets the primary stress:

```
              /      /      ^    /
a white house: white + house = white house
```

In this example, an adjective with primary stress is demoted to secondary stress when the adjective is placed before a noun. A difference can be noted when the actual result of the formula is a compound word phonologically but not orthographically (i. e., a compound in sound but not in spelling). Such is the case for the name of the house where the U. S. President lives. By rights, the *White House* ought to be spelled the *Whitehouse*:

$$/ \quad / \quad \quad / \quad \wedge$$
white + house = whitehouse

A similar variation in stress placement distinguishes a *black bird* (any old bird which happens to be black) from a *blackbird* (a particular species of black bird):

$$\wedge \quad / \quad \quad / \quad \wedge$$
black bird *versus* blackbird

Exercise 1.4
Directions: Assign stress to the words below:

    blackjack
    tire tool
    a big deal
    newsroom
    a new room
    springboard
    doorway
    old lady
    yellow jacket
    skyjack
    keepsake

This business of stress assignment, however, can get very complicated. A further refinement of the rules would specify that when the main stress of a word is demoted, the other stresses of the word are also demoted. Take for example the phrase *classroom teacher*. We start with three elements, *class, room,* and *teacher:*

Compound Stress Rule

$$/ \quad \quad / \quad \quad \quad / \quad \wedge$$
class + room = classroom

Nuclear Stress Rule with Additional Demotion

$$/ \quad \wedge \quad \quad / \quad \quad \quad \wedge \quad \backslash \quad \quad /$$
classroom + teacher = classroom teacher

At this point, you may be having considerable trouble hearing the differences among these syllables. It may be difficult for you to decide if *class* or *teacher* should get more stress. If we are looking for a noun phrase (a group of words with a noun as its head), *teacher* will get the primary stress; if we want a compound word (and such is possible), *class* will get the primary stress. This last example also shows us that we have at least four levels of stress in English. Linguists once argued this widely (cf. Gleason and LaPalombara, but note Lieberman), but in practice we probably have a great many levels made in a great many gradations. At any rate, the fourth level of stress is called simply *no stress* or for the sake of consistency *quarternary* stress. It is often symbolized with an *x*.

As we have seen, intention is important, and the analysis of the last example has placed everyday considerations aside. It is simply not important for English speakers to be able to hear the differences between *class* and *teacher* for there to be a meaningful difference. However, as academics we often sit around looking for minute differences that become meaningful to us. Fine gradations of stress placement, however, can make the difference between the following two expressions: *a lighthousekeeper* and *a light housekeeper*. The first expression describes someone whose job it is to keep a light going in a tower to warn ships of hazardous waters; the second is a maid of sorts who does not do heavy work or who may not weigh very much. The stress assignment of each expression can vary depending on how we hear the words, but the difference between the two expressions depends heavily on where we place the primary stress:

> x /   ^   \ x
> a lighthousekeeper *or*

> x /   \   ^ x
> a lighthousekeeper *(depending on the order in which we combine)*

> x ^   /   ^ x
> a light housekeeper *or*

> x ^   /   \ x
> a light housekeeper *or*

> x \   /   ^ x
> a light housekeeper *(depending on what we hear)*

Exercise 1.5
Directions: Assign stress to the following expressions. Be prepared to defend your
answers.

  elevator operator
  dictionary editor
  heavy bookkeeping
  amenable institutions
  bookkeeping exercises

  The assignment of stress to a word may also depend on its function in a clause.
In general, we can say that stress is thrown to the right in a clause. Thus the verbal
complement is normally emphasized:

  /
I want some bread.

      /
He is angry.

              /
I am going to town.

It is possible to assign stress levels to other words in a sentence, but these assignments
are open to interpretation. There is a tradition among scholars, however, to regard
some words as grammatically more important and thus more important in terms of
stress assignment. The parts of speech are thus divided up into *major category words*
and *minor category words*. Major category words are nouns, adjectives, adverbs, and
sometimes verbs; minor category words are articles, qualifiers, pronouns, conjunctions,
prepositions, and sometimes verbs. Major category words tend to get primary or
secondary stress on their main-stressed syllables, and minor category words usually
get tertiary or quarternary stress on theirs. Using such a scheme and some intuition,
it is possible to give the following stress assignments to the first example given above:

      ^   \   /
I want some bread.

Following the stipulation above about throwing stress to the right, I have assigned
primary stress to the noun object of the verb. The verb seems to command some
prominence in the sentence and receives the secondary stress; the determiner *some*

could perhaps receive secondary stress, but in this reading it has received tertiary stress. Although these assignments seem plausible, they are not the only assignments possible. Other readings would depend on the intention of the speaker. We could emphasize the subject by giving it primary stress:

> / ^ \ /
> I want some bread.

Similarly, we could emphasize other words in the sentence by giving them primary stress—the configurations would all depend on the point we were trying to make about the speaker's desire for a bakery product:

> \ / \ /
> I want some bread.

> ^ \ / ^
> I want some bread.

> / / / /
> I want some bread.

In the last example, we have the utterance of someone yelling. We would probably give him some bread.

It is further possible to assign stress to words in longer utterances, but it would be easier—or more valid at any rate—to make these assignments on a sentence recorded from actual speech. But for the sake of example I offer the following sentence with my own prejudices for stress assignment thrown in:

> x   \   x / \ x x / x / \   x
> Although the cat hated the rat, the dog found that

> x / x x \ x ^ x x / x
> the rat was an entertaining companion.

Other readers may come up with slightly different readings, but I believe that the reading I have given above will be possible (if not probable) in a native speaker's performance of the sentence.

Exercise 1.6
Directions: Give stress assignments to the words in the sentences below. Indicate what other stress assignments would be possible given the proper context.

1. The boy fell down the stairs.
2. He hit the ball.
3. I would like some chocolate pie.
4. When I got to the dance, I felt moved to shake my legs.
5. Ringing in the New Year, we partied till we puked.

A further complication arises in the assignment of stress to words in clauses. This complication concerns the melody of speech: *pitch*. Although we do not know much at all about the complexities of pitch in English sentences, we do know that we use it in general patterns and for emphasis and other emotional effects. The same linguists that gave us the notion of four levels of stress gave us the notion of four levels of pitch. To symbolize pitch levels we use the numerals *1, 2, 3*, and *4*. *1* designates the lowest pitch; *4*, the highest; and *2* and *3* levels in between. A "normal" declarative sentence is said to start at *2* and to rise to *3* before dropping off to *1* at the end of the sentence. Here is an example:

/
[2]I want some [3]bread.[1]

We could also symbolize these levels of pitch with musical or quasi-musical notation:

I want some bread.

A line indicating a contour of pitch may also work:

I want some bread.

The pattern illustrated above is the general contour of declarative sentences, but the pattern may vary according to the desire of the speaker to give emphasis or other emotional coloring to his speech. An angry or frustrated person may break into something like this:

     [2]I [4]want [2]some [4]bread.[1]

An interesting aspect of general pitch patterns is that they vary for the two main kinds of questions we have in English. One kind of question asks for specific kinds of information. Since these kinds of questions use interrogative words like *what* or *why*, they have come to be called WH-Questions. WH-Questions use declarative sentence intonation (2-3-1):

     [2]What do you [3]want?[1]

The other kind of question that we have in English is the Yes/No Question. This kind of question asks for a response of *yes* or *no*, and it uses a pitch pattern of 2-3. The pitch rises from the beginning and trails off upward at the end:

     [2]Do you want some bread?[3]

When we try to assign pitch, we run into some of the same problems we do when we assign stress. When we have a recording of a speaker, we all find it much easier to agree on what occurs in a sentence. In a sentence out of context, we can find much to disagree about since we may have differing senses of the meaning of a sentence and the best way to deliver the sentence for the intended effect. An interesting experience in this regard is to attend an audition for a play in which different people are given the same lines to deliver. The differences in pitch (and stress, for that matter) often become criteria for judging who is the best actor or actress.

Exercise 1.7
Directions: Assign pitch levels to the following sentences. Indicate where and how the levels could be modified.

    1. I want to go home.
    2. Go home!

3. Do you like raw fish?
4. What is your name?
5. When you finally get to the stadium, you should turn left and go down the road until you hit the interstate.

As we saw above, stress and pitch are related. The word or syllable with the strongest stress also has the highest pitch. This is not to say that stress and pitch are absolutely interchangeable, but the temptation to interchange them has been delectable for some scholars. Experiments on pairs like *permit* (noun) and *permit* (verb) have shown, however, that pitch and other aspects of speech may be determinants of stress (Bolinger, Fry, Lieberman). In fact, there are four aspects of spoken syllables that we may hear as stress or accent: *loudness, length, pitch change,* and *expectation.* We shall treat each in its turn.

Many scholars have and still do consider stress to be mainly an item of loudness (or in acoustic terms, *amplitude*). Relative stress and relative loudness are related, and experiments do show that English speakers can hear the difference between the two forms of *permit* if machines are used to control the other determinants of stress. However, it should come as no surprise that loudness is not the best determinant of stress. A common problem we have is realizing when we are being too loud or soft in our speech. We have all met someone who talks too loud, and we have all lived through the unnerving experience of trying to hear someone who will not speak up. As it turns out, we are not very good at controlling how we stress words according to loudness, and we are not very good at hearing differences signaled by loudness. Something must be said, however, in defense of scholars who believe in the kinesthetic power of poetic meter and who believe that the pulse of the verse makes us feel the reader's efforts to louden or soften his voice. But loudness is nevertheless not a reliable indicator of stress.

A more reliable indicator appears to be *duration.* Some scholars—especially scholars who have studied Latin verse, which depends on the alternation of long and short syllables—have felt for a long time that duration was an important part of English versification. The experiments mentioned above showed that duration was much more effective than loudness in signaling the difference between the two forms of *permit.* A careful listener may also perceive how important duration can be in English poetry (Baker), but we will have much more to say about that later. For the time being, however, you might play with the word *permit* as best you can to see how duration and loudness can be varied in pronouncing its forms.

The most reliable indicator of stress, however, is pitch change. The reader will please note that I said *pitch change* and not *pitch* itself. Pitch itself is not a particularly good device for signaling stress, for although we can vary the pitch from syllable to syllable in a word like *permit,* the listener becomes confused when the word is out of context. A low tone followed by a high tone or vice versa does not mean anything to an English speaker. A pitch change within a syllable, on the other hand, is a very useful device for signaling stress. When one syllable has no pitch change and the other syllable does, the difference between the syllables is very noticeable. The syllable with the pitch change draws much attention to itself, and thus it is perceived as having stress. When I first read about pitch change as important in signaling stress, I must admit that I thought about the whole claim as somewhat of a curiosity. However, after living in the Southeast for a while, I can honestly say that yes, indeed, pitch change in a syllable is an important part of English stress. Southerners regularly use pitch changes in syllables (or what may sound like a group of syllables to outsiders) to signal stress. For outsiders this general tendency sounds like a "drawl." An effective way of discovering this process is to pronounce the two forms of *permit* with a rising-falling melody on the stressed syllable.

The first three means of signaling or perceiving stress are physical facts of language. These aspects of speech can be isolated and measured in some way by machines. The fourth means of signaling and perceiving stress is *psychological*. In short, we hear what we want to hear. A commonly noted problem in factory quality control is that when people have to inspect thousands of items running by on a conveyor belt, they often miss seeing mistakes. Such people are often grouped in twos, but they still miss major mistakes in the products that they inspect. Perhaps you know what I am talking about from the experience of doing some tedious, repetitious task. An obvious example for a college student is proofreading. How many times have you misspelled a word or made a subject/verb agreement error because you just were not paying attention? You knew what you were saying, and a minor letter or two were inconsequential in view of what you were trying to say. A fact of language is that we make "mistakes" as we talk or that we have trouble hearing what has been said. We have the ability, however, to fill in what has not been said or what has not been heard based on what we know about the speaker or the language and its operation. A mispronounced word will not throw us if we are able to figure out what was intended from the context. Thus we are able to provide stress assignments that may have been garbled by the speaker. In the scansion of poetry, we may hear a pattern of stresses where, in terms of linguistic reality, there may be no clear pattern.

Although we may not think very often about things such as pitch and stress, I hope that you can now see that these aspects of speech are real—in the sense of perceivable—and that their behavior is reasonably predictable. Because these aspects are predictable and because they are not always phonemic, they become at once something for poets to use to organize language. We can discover this organization with a minimum amount of labor, and this discovery can delight us with surprise since these aspects of speech are usually not clearly organized in obvious patterns. We can say that in some ways there is a rhythm to speech and that stress timing is a part of the repertoire of every English speaker, but the poetic organization of stress tends to be very regular. The regularity of this organization becomes interesting in itself and gives the poet something from which he can depart to gain attention.

References and Suggested Reading

Baker, Sheridan. "English Meter *Is* Quantitative." *College English* 21 (1960): 309-15.

Bolinger, Dwight L. "A Theory of Pitch Accent in English." *Word* 14 (1958): 109-49.

Fry, D. B. "Duration and Intensity as Physical Correlates of Linguistic Stress." *Journal of the Acoustical Society of America* 27 (1955): 765-68.

—. "Experiments in the Perception of Stress." *Language and Speech* 1 (1958): 126-52.

Gleason, H. A., Jr. *An Introduction to Descriptive Linguistics*. Rev. ed. New York: Holt, Rinehart and Winston, 1961.

Halle, Morris, and Samuel J. Keyser. *English Stress: Its Form, Its Growth, and Its Role in Verse*. New York: Harper and Row, 1971.

LaPalombara, Lyda E. *An Introduction to Grammar: Traditional, Structural, Transformational*. Cambridge, Mass.: Winthrop Publishers, 1976.

Lieberman, Philip. "On the Acoustic Basis of the Perception of Intonation by Linguists." *Word* 21 (1965): 40-54.

Two: Rhythm and Meter in Modern English

In the last chapter we noted that expectation is an important part of perception. Without expectation, one of the most delightful experiences in life would be meaningless: rhythm. Rhythm is the perception of a recurrent action or pattern. In *The Science of English Verse* (62), Sidney Lanier tells us that we can experience rhythm with all of our senses. In his elegant way, he asks us to imagine a rose—a pleasant thought. He says that if we wave the rose in front of our eyes with some regularity in time, we experience rhythm in sight. If we wave the rose past one of our ears, we experience rhythm in sound. Lanier also tells us that if we wave the rose past our noses, we will know rhythm in smell. If we alternately place the rose in our mouth or stroke it across our skin, we have rhythm in taste or feeling.

While stimulated by external things, rhythm—as St. Augustine of Hippo once explained (1163 ff.)—is nevertheless a mental process. In order for there to be rhythm in any meaningful sense, something must be perceived and remembered. If, for example, a rhythm is occurring in time, memory makes it possible for us to know that something has happened and that it is happening again and again as the case may be. If a rhythm is spatial (a more modern conception), we perceive a pattern in our visual experience. Rhythm, in short, is a mental experience stimulated by the senses.

Rhythm is very important to us. Our hearts beat with a regular rhythm in time, and we find out that babies and the young of animals find it comforting to hear facsimiles of heart beats. We make our clocks of rhythmic devices of various sorts, and we live our lives according to large chunks of these temporal rhythms. We live in a world where rhythm is marked by the movements of the sun, the moon, and the seasons, and we observe that even animals and plants are affected by and create rhythms of various sorts. Appropriately, rhythm forms an important part of all of our arts. Temporal rhythm is central to our music, which organizes tones against a background of pulses. Dance is movement organized in a temporal rhythm. The visual and plastic arts of painting and sculpture also use rhythm, although not temporal rhythm. Patterns are often important in art works, and these patterns are essentially rhythms in space. In some works the patterns are obtrusive, but in many others the rhythm is subtle but nonetheless there. The rhythm in these kinds of art moves the eye in certain directions and urges us to focus on certain parts of the work. Similarly, poetry, as temporal and spatial art, is generally rhythmic.

The importance of rhythm to us cannot be emphasized enough. Rhythm in many ways governs our working lives, and a common way of escaping the monotony of our daily lives is to lose ourselves in rhythm. For example, I love to drive with the radio on, and I often do not care what kind of music is playing. I tap along with the music, and I even sway in my seat. When I am in a good mood at home, I dance around to the music, and often to the misery of my wife I dance around her and pull her around the kitchen floor. I have lived next to college students, and I have observed that they live in a bombardment of rhythm. They come driving up to the house with a tapeplayer blaring and then turn on the stereo as soon as they walk into the house. The rhythm and its obvious release is so important to them that I can hear the drum beat and the pounding of the bass in my house even when their house and my house are closed up for the winter. As a part of the ritual, one of the students will play the drums along with the record, sometimes playing the same record over and over again intoxicated with the repetition of the thump-thumpy-thump. This same kind of release from the drudgery of life also fills up dance halls with people hungry for escape. You can find people of all ages swaying and jumping to the beat of the music—and everyone seems to be having fun.

There are also ritualistic purposes for rhythm. Many churches make use of music in ceremonies, and some use music that is very close to what one may hear in a jumping night place. We have all seen movies of primitive peoples who use overpowering music to accompany their religious rituals and to build reverential awe to an orgiastic level. Rhythm is also an integral part of such rituals as marching. Marching soldiers or high-school bands step to the beat of the drums, and the parade watchers, the enemy, or the fans are appropriately stirred by the feeling that the marching people are very powerful. This ritualistic sense of power is probably no more evident in our society than at sporting events, where we indulge in tribal behavior. Spectator sports like football and basketball are played to the accompaniment of incantations. Young women in colorful and skimpy outfits perform mystic, rhythmic spells designed to embolden the spirits of their teams and crush the spirits of their opponents. And although cheerleading has become a much more self-centered activity than it was when I was in high school, there is still some attempt to elicit the spiritual power of rhythm among the fans. The fans and the cheerleaders engage in a chant, feeling that the power of their words will be transferred to the action on the field. As I remember my high school days, I can still feel the power when we would all chant as loud as we could at a football game:

Hit'em again! Hit'em again!
Harder, harder!
Hit'em again! Hit'em again!
Harder, harder!

Although we probably did not realize what we were doing, we were calling on the power of rhythm to sway our emotions and the emotions of the opposing side. We hoped our rhythm had more power than the rhythm of our opponents.

Rhythm then is often our link with a prehistoric past. The depth of our connection with rhythm, however, is not often something that we realize. A common example given of our need to perceive rhythm concerns the mechanical clock. Most of us assume that the clock goes "tick-tock." That is, we think we hear pulses of unevenly accented beats. If we are careful in our listening, though, we will hear not "tick-tock-tick-tock" but "tick-tick-tick-tick." There is essentially no difference between the ticks on the clock, but we organize the repetition into recognizable beats and off-beats. These beats and off-beats are projections of our minds. We are simply creatures of rhythm.

Although it would be interesting to look at rhythm in a general study, we must at some point get on to Chaucer. The best way, I believe, to do this is to become more familiar with the rhythms of Modern English poetry, and in this chapter we will look closely at how rhythm works in Modern English. Since we can more generally agree on the pronunciation of modern words, it will be easier to learn some principles of scansion with some familiar texts. Then we can tackle the problems of scanning poetry in a language that is for all intents and purposes dead outside of our imaginations. Let us begin with some very familiar lines.

I am sure that many of you are familiar with Robert Frost's famous poem "Stopping by Woods on a Snowy Evening." Although Frost is a modern poet, he prefers to write in traditional meters. Frost said that writing poetry without meter was like playing tennis without a net. At any rate, here is a line from his famous poem:

Between the woods and frozen lake. (Frost 194)

Experience with Frost or having a good ear would quickly alert us that Frost has provided a line that reads somewhat rhythmically—i. e., we have a recurrent pattern here. However, some people may have some trouble hearing the pattern, and a little analysis is required to discover the rhythm. Since the words of poetry do not often follow normal word-order rules, we cannot always rely on our intuitions for making stress assignments, but we can sort out many of the difficulties if we proceed methodically.

What we do is take each word and phrase at a time and then put together the things we find into a pattern. It is often helpful to start with multisyllabic words since they come with ready-made stress patterns. The first word should give us little trouble. The normal pronunciation of *between* in Modern English places stronger stress on the second syllable than on the first syllable:

        x   /
        Between

Another word we can look at is *frozen*; it is stressed on the first syllable:

        / x
        frozen

The next step is to look at monosyllabic words in grammatical structures: phrases. In this line *the woods* is the obvious choice, and remembering the nuclear stress rule, we can assign stress, throwing the primary stress to the right:

        x   /
        the woods

Using the same rule, we can build on what we have discovered about *frozen* and place it before lake:

        / x   /   ^ x /
        frozen + lake > frozen lake

Earlier we gave primary stress to the second syllable of *between,* but in context we may want to demote the primary stress of the preposition:

        x /   x /   x \   x /
        Between + the woods > Between the woods

Someone may ask why we do not give secondary stress to the second syllable of *Between,* and I will grant that this is a good question. However, since we are following the traditional notion that prepositions are minor category words and do not receive much stress, we give only tertiary stress to the stressed syllable of *Between* and thus leave the secondary stress for the demoted adjectival *frozen.* But since the words are separated from each other, it is actually hard to hear any difference between the syllables in question. This objection will lead us to a conception of meter, but for now let us continue our methodical study of this line.

    The only word we have left is *and.* It is a minor category word, so we can expect that it will not normally receive much stress, although there are times when we can stress this conjunction very heavily for emphasis. Here, however, emphasis is not motivated, and it is safe to give the word very little stress. It certainly would get less stress than *woods*, a noun, and *frozen*, the demoted adjectival past participle. The results of our analysis produce the following:

```
   x  \    x  /    x   ^  x  /
Between the woods and frozen lake
```

So far we have been looking at the trees, and now we need to stand back and see the forest, which is actually easier to see than the trees. As we read the line, we conclude that we have a pattern: the syllables are arranged in an order of weaker-stronger stress from the beginning to the end of the line. We could look at the line as a series of hills and valleys of stress. Some hills here are higher than others, but a basic pattern is operating.

We could proceed deductively through the other lines of the poem, and we could be here for another fifty pages or so to learn something that we can easily generalize. Frost is working with a meter in this poem. Meter is a kind of rhythm about which much has been written and about which much has been argued. But very simply put, meter is an abstract pattern (Lewis, Malof, and Wimsatt and Beardsley). The poet thinks of the abstract pattern as he writes, and he tries to make the stresses of the words he chooses follow the pattern he has in his mind. Sometimes the pattern he has in his mind is temporal—even musical in its rhythmic demands; at other times the pattern is simply a pattern of weaker-stronger and so on. Our job as prosodists is to discover the pattern the poet had in mind and to see how he followed the pattern. We can also make suggestions about how the poem should be read, but our primary concern is to find out what the pattern is and how the words form it.

A traditional way of indicating how the pattern works in a line of verse is based on the practice of ancient Greek and Latin poets. For better or worse, educated people until the present century were required to learn Latin generally and Greek less generally. As a result, they were exposed to the rules and methods of Greek and Latin prosody. Although Greek and Latin classical verse does not use stress as an organizing agent, English poets and scholars have used the Greek and Roman patterns as models for English verse organized by stress patterns. Attempts are often made, however, to substitute some other system to account for the rhythmic structure of traditional English verse. The systems often provide interesting views of English verse, but the simplest method of accounting for the verse is the identification of the meter that the poet was thinking of when he wrote the poem. This kind of endeavor is often cited as circular, but in this case, circularity is not a condemnation. The poet thought of a pattern and wrote according to the pattern; our job is to discover the pattern in the words. Once a fellow student in one of my classes complained that a critic was circular in an argument; a disgruntled teacher replied with a remark that applies in our study of meter: "Yes, the argument is circular, but it circulates the right way."

Following our circle, we can read Frost's line in a couple of ways. A simple one is to see the pattern of weaker-stronger as continuing in an organic way across the entire line:

```
x  /    x  /    x   / x  /
x  \    x  /    x  ^ x  /
```
Between the woods and frozen lake

The symbols just above the line of verse repeat the reading we argued for above. Above these marks we have a new set of symbols. This new set of symbols reduces our original reading with its secondary and tertiary stresses to simple contrasts of weaker-stronger. Some may argue that this kind of reduction smoothes over too many differences, but in actuality all the reduction really does is identify the pattern that Frost may have had in his head as he wrote. If he had tried to write the poem, however, in contrasts of quarternary and primary stresses, the poem would soon have become dull. It is hard to continue writing or reading a poem with the stress pattern of a line like the following:

The cat, the dog, the fish, the goat

Such a production would soon become deadening in its effect. The Frost line cited above does use the same *general* pattern that this line does, but Frost had either the luck or the sense to vary the intensity of the stress contrasts.

The classically based meter that Frost uses in the line we have been discussing is called iambic tetrameter. *Iambic* means that the general stress pattern of the line is weaker-stronger. A unit of this combination of weaker-stronger syllables is called a foot. *Tetrameter* means that there are four feet to the line (*tetra* 'four'; *metron* 'measure'). Using this "classical" description as our model, we can scan the line like this:

```
x  /  |  x  /   | x   /| x  /
```
Between the woods and frozen lake

The vertical line drawn between the groups of weaker-stronger units is the foot-marker.

"Classical" scansion has come under fire in the last few decades, mainly because of the notion of the foot. Prosodists have been concerned in many cases with how the lines they are scanning should be read. The important word here is *line*. These prosodists have been looking at whole lines and the patterns of stress that make up the line structure. This kind of investigation is very interesting and useful, but it leaves out the foot as both a compositional and an explanatory device. The usual objection to the foot marker is that the foot does not exist. We can agree that the foot does not exist as a syntactic or morphological device per se, but it may often have relationships with syntactic or morphological structures. But even when these special relationships do not exist, we cannot necessarily claim that the foot does not exist. The foot is part of the abstract pattern that the poet uses in composition. The mistake of many prosodists is to believe too dogmatically in the existence of the foot as an independent phonological entity. While the foot does describe in a rough way a phonological reality, a foot in a given line is not an independent entity—it is part of the whole pattern of stresses in the line. However, the foot is independent as an abstraction.

Let us use a new example to illustrate the last claim. Here is a line of iambic pentameter from Shakespeare's *A Midsummer Night's Dream*:

The dove pursues the griffon, the mild hind (II, i, 232)

Since I have already told you what the line is, you may already have guessed how the line should be scanned. You know that *iambic* means that the line should have feet composed of syllables in the stress pattern of weaker-stronger. If you know Greek roots, you could guess that *pentameter* means that there will be five feet in the line (*penta* 'five'). If we tried to apply our linguistic levels of stress to the line, we might come up with something like this:

        x /   x \   x / x   x ^   /
        The dove pursues the griffon, the mild hind

If we then try to see the alternating pattern without invoking the foot as a compositional or scanning device, we may run into a problem. The weaker-stronger pattern works well with the first part of the line, but it runs into trouble with the end of the line:

        x /   x /   x / x   ? ?   /
        The dove pursues the griffon, the mild hind

One solution to the problem is to go with our ears (which are generally trustworthy) and give stress where stress seems to go even if the pattern is disturbed:

        x /   x /   x / x   x /   /
        The dove pursues the griffon, the mild hind

For some readers this is a perfectly acceptable reading, and I think that it does justice to our ears. However, the reading obscures the meter of the poem.

If we use the foot to understand how the line is put together, the line still follows the iambic pattern. If we were poets constructing a line of iambic pentameter, we would be thinking in terms of twos. We would write and collect words and syllables according to the pattern we were following. As we wrote (and we can assume as Shakespeare wrote), we would choose words and syllables according to our pattern, and the first two syllables would fit our pattern of weaker-stronger: *The dove*. Here we have an unstressed article and the heavily stressed noun that the article modifies. The two monosyllables make up our first foot. The second foot is filled entirely by the word *pursues*, a word of French origin with its accent on the second syllable— another iamb. The next foot is made up of the article *the* and the first syllable of *griffon*. *Griffon*, a noun, is stressed heavily on its first syllable and commands more stress than the article preceding it. We thus have another iamb. The next two syllables give us a problem: they are both unstressed. Similarly, the last two syllables both receive stress, although of different levels.

And this last concession is the crux of the situation. We start the line with an iambic pattern that is fairly straight forward, and if we are careful, we can see that according to our nuclear stress rule, *hind* will command more prominence than *mild*. With our handy division of the line into feet of two syllables, we have solved the foot-scansion of four of the five feet. The foot with the two unstressed syllables, however, is still a problem. If we wish to preserve the iambic pattern of the line, we have two solutions to offer. One, we can simply argue that although the syllables are unstressed, they do not have the same stress assignment. Many prosodists will argue that two contiguous syllables simply never have the same level of stress. The syllables will be different because of their syntactic, morphological, or phonological structure. Following this type of argument, we could claim that *the* receives more stress than *-on*: *the* is a function word that gives definiteness to the noun phrase that follows it while *-on* is merely an unstressed, meaningless second syllable of a dissyllabic word; therefore, *-on* may scurry by in pronunciation as a syllabic consonant while *the* gains prominence because of its syntactic function and because of its apparently greater burden in pronunciation. Two, even if we do not grant the preceding linguistic arguments, we can turn to expectation. We have been hearing a pattern in the line, and when we come to syllables which otherwise have the same stress, the pattern that we have causes us to demote one syllable and promote the other.

You will remember what we said about the ticking of the clock. We have a hard time hearing a recurring tick as the same sound over and over again: we soon turn the monotony into a rhythm of "tick-tock." Given our propensity to hear rhythm, it is very easy (and very justifiable) to scan the line with five iambs:

        x / │ x / │ x /│ x   /│ x   /
    The dove pursues the griffon, the mild hind

The mistake that is often made in regard to such lines is assuming that the feet are in some way equal in pronunciation. While there have apparently been some very stiff prosodists who would view such an aberration as part of poetic art, it is not fair to say that this feeling is general. All the foot does is allow us to weigh syllables in composition (or conversely in scansion). The result for pronuciation may be as clear as the Frost line we examined in detail above or as the line I made up, or the result may be the rather interesting line that we have been examining from Shakespeare. Scansion with feet, we must remember, is not a prescription for performance. It is the identification of the abstract pattern that the poet may have held in his mind as he wrote a particular line of verse.

Other foot prosodists may argue, however, that the line should be scanned with a double last foot ($x\ x\ /\ /$) or a combination of a pyrrhic ($x\ x$) and spondaic foot ($/\ /$):

> x / | x / | x /| x   x   /   /
> The dove pursues the griffon, the mild hind

> x / | x / | x   /| x   x| /   /
> The dove pursues the griffon, the mild hind

My only argument against these readings is that they obscure the abstract pattern of the meter. These readings are true to how the lines sound, but they fail to show us how the particular configuration of the line develops from the basic pattern. Actually, our choice for scansion in this instance is a matter of taste—taste, that is, based on defensible lines of reason. These latter readings follow a rhythmically oriented conception of meter—a performance-oriented model; the scansion I prefer is oriented more toward a compositional model.

But this is not to say that poetry has nothing to do with rhythm. No, it has much to do with rhythm, but in our search for rhythm we must beware of leaving aside the compositional basis of the line. Nevertheless, the rhythmic aspect of these lines we have been playing with can use some attention.

The problem with relying too heavily on rhythmic scansions of verse is that we soon leave the description of the meter for a prescription for performance. Some verse, however, was meant to be read with a musical rhythm. Obvious examples are ballads. Ballads were written to be sung, and they typically have a pattern of four lines: the first and third lines have four stresses and the second and fourth lines have three stresses. While there may be definite foot patterns in the lines, often there are not. In addition, ballads may count on heavy promotion and demotion to make the rhythm of the lines clear. Musical rhythm rules in the ballad whether it is sung or recited:

```
  x   /   x   /   x  / x x /
```
"Mak haste, mak haste, my mirry men all,

```
 x    /   x   /   x  /
```
Our guid schip sails the morn."

```
 x / x /   x / x /
```
"O say na sae, my master deir,

```
 x x / x /   x   /
```
For I feir a deadlie storme." ("Sir Patrick Spens" in Perrine 556)

Although other scansions of these lines are possible, the scansion given above is probable for a performance of the poem. A thing to notice is how the rhythm runs roughshod over the linguistic structure in the promotion of adjectives over nouns. The variations in the number of unstressed syllables is another thing to watch. The pattern of syllables does not in and of itself generate the rhythm but is subject itself to the rhythm. Further, in this type of verse there is a tendency to observe musical measures so much so that in the lines above we would tap out a fourth beat after the three-beat lines. A musical scansion would illustrate these problems a little more clearly:

"Mak haste, mak haste, my mirry men all,

Our guid schip sails the morn."

"O say na sae, my master deir,

For I feir a deadlie storme."

Although we chose to use cut time for the above lines, other time signatures could have been used. Indeed, the variability of the application of rhythmic structures is important. We do not want to deny what musical or temporal rhythms in a poem can do for our reading, but we must be shy of the blind application of musical rhythms as standards for metrical scansion.

If you have had experience with a particularly irreverent department of English, you may have already heard someone sing Robert Frost's "Stopping by Woods on a Snowy Evening." I know of at least two melodies that will work with the poem— neither one of them particularly appropriate for Frost's subject. One is a butchered version of *The William Tell Overture*; the other is a very awkward version of "Fernando's Hideaway," a song from the popular musical *The Pajama Game*. Either way the result is ludicrous because the inappropriate rhythm is thrust upon the innocent poem in a perverse reading. While such readings are possible, they are not probable as justifiable readings of the poem as we assume the author may have intended it to be read. As it turns out, we have a record of Frost reading this poem, and you will not be surprised to find out that Frost uses neither of these abominable rhythms. We may disagree over how good Frost's reading of the poem is as a performance, but we must agree that common sense and good taste must rule our metrical readings. In short, we have to decide if the poem in question is musical or metrical and then proceed from there. In the case of Frost and Shakespeare, our decision is to go with the metrical scansion and to leave aside the musical one.

However, a careful reader should pay some attention to the temporal or musical rhythms that may develop in a poem. Just because a writer may have had a simple foot prosody in mind when he wrote does not necessarily mean that the poem will not have musical tendencies. One way of talking about musical rhythm or temporal rhythm is to talk about *isochronism*. *Iso-* means equal; *chron-* means time; the whole expression refers to rhythm based on nearly equal durations of time. A claim often made about the verse of poets who have traditionally been called writers of iambic pentameter is that they actually write in four-stress or four-beat rhythm. And there is something to be said in favor of this observation. It is very easy to follow the major stresses of lines of iambic pentameter and come up with lines of four stresses that can be read with isochronous measures:

> /   /   /   /
> My hounds are bred out of the Spartan kind:
> /   /   /   /
> So flewed, so sanded, and their heads are hung
> /   /   /   /
> With tears that sweep away the morning dew.

(*A Midsummer Night's Dream*, IV, i, 118-120)

Certainly such a reading is possible, but it obscures the major compositional fact of the line—five feet. The first line probably contains a reversed foot—something we haven't talked about. A reversed foot in iambic poetry is a *trochee* (a foot with the pattern of stronger-weaker) substituted for the normal iamb. Allowing this substitution (and it is a kind of substitution that has been common in English metrical poetry), we can easily scan the lines according to the iambic pentameter pattern:

```
  x /    |x    / | /   x | x  / | x   /
My hounds are bred out of the Spartan kind:
```

```
  x /   | x / | x  / | x  /   | x  /
So flewed, so sanded, and their heads are hung
```

```
  x  /   | x   / | x / | x / | x   /
With tears that sweep away the morning dew.
```

The first reading emphasizes the rhythm of the lines at the expense of the meter; the second emphasizes the meter at the expense of the rhythm. Thus I think it becomes important to do two things when scanning verse: one, identify the meter; two, explore the rhythmic patterns that develop from the lines in a reasonable reading.

Not all lines of verse are going to feel the same even though they may all be written in the same meter. Milton, for example, in *Paradise Lost* follows a fairly regular metrical scheme, but the scheme allows him to produce lines of vastly differing rhythmic qualities. He offers us the perfectly plain line in which metrical and linguistic stress run together:

```
  x      / |x  / | x   / | x  / | x  /
And swims or sinks, or wades, or creeps, or flies  (II, 950)
```

He can also create a marvelously heavy line which stretches our capacity to understand the line as metrical. The following line is metrical by means of syllables compared in feet with all the aspects of burden taken into consideration:

```
  x    /   | x    / | x   / |x    / |x  /
Rocks, Caves, Lakes, Fens, Bogs, Dens, and shades of Death  (I, 621)
```

Illusion as much as anything works to make this line metrical, but when we weigh *Rocks* against *Caves* we sense that the voiced final consonants make *Caves* seem to have more burden than *Rocks*. The sequence of *Lakes, Fens* repeats the same metrical trick, and the next sequence of *Bogs, Dens* frustrates this pattern as a new pattern based on the rhyme of *Fens* and *Dens* gives *Dens* metrical prominence over *Bogs*. In addition, the expectation of the pattern of weaker-stronger makes us hear the second word in each pair as prominent, although the words carry more or less equal linguistic stress. However, the rhythmic effect of the line is far different from that of the plain line above. While a heavy-handed scansion of three spondees is slightly deaf in its approach, a musical scansion might give a more felicitous rendering of the line and its burden:

Rocks, Caves, Lakes, Fens, Bogs, Dens, and shades of Death

This scansion prescribes the reading we hear and negates the minor differences in perceived syllable length. It respects the importance of nouns by giving them half notes but observes the meter with accents.

This chapter has illustrated a few principles of English versification. Although we have covered much, we have essentially scratched only the surface of the considerations we ought to make when we scan Chaucer's verse. However, it is time to get on to Chaucer. When new considerations need to be introduced, we will turn to Chaucer for examples. You are now ready to treat the master of our interest.

Exercise 2.1

Shakespeare often uses different meters in his plays for different effects. Identify the meters of the following lines and scan them. Then discuss the possible rhythmic performances of the lines. Which lines lend themselves to musical readings? Which don't? Why don't they?

a. You spotted snakes with double tongue,
        Thorny hedgehogs, be not seen;
    Newts and blindworms, do no wrong,
        Come not near our Fairy Queen.
            (*A Midsummer Night's Dream*, II, ii, 9-12.)

b. Your wrongs do set a scandal on my sex.
    We cannot fight for love, as men may do;
    We should be wooed, and were not made to woo.
            (*A Midsummer Night's Dream*, II, i, 240-42)

Exercise 2.2

Here is an exercise in irreverence. Go through a sophomore literary anthology and see how many poems you can find that can be sung to popular melodies. Some good ones to try out are "The Yellow Rose of Texas" and "My Bonnie Lies over the Ocean." (A good place to start is with Emily Dickinson; many of her poems can be sung to the first tune.) Also see what poems lend themselves to the melodies of rhythm and blues. With a little repetition in the manner of a blues song, many lines of iambic pentameter make acceptable words for the rhythm and blues.

References and Suggested Reading

Augustine, Bishop of Hippo. *De Musica.* In *Patrologiae Cursus Completus.* Ed. J.-P. Migne. Paris: Garnier, 1877. XXXII, 1081-1194.

Frost, Robert. *Robert Frost's Poems.* New York: Washington Square Press, 1971.

Lanier, Sidney. *The Science of English Verse.* New York: Charles Scribner's Sons, 1898.

Lewis, C. S. "Metre." *Review of English Literature* 1 (1960): 45-50.

Malof, Joseph. "The Artifice of Scansion." *English Journal* 54 (1965): 857-60, 871.

Milton, John. *John Milton: Complete Poems and Major Prose.* Ed. Merritt Y. Hughes. New York: Macmillan, 1985.

Perrine, Laurence. *Literature: Structure, Sound, and Sense.* New York: Harcourt Brace Jovanovich, 1978.

Shakespeare, William. *A Midsummer Night's Dream.* Ed. Madeleine Doran. New York: Penguin, 1971.

Wimsatt, W. K., Jr., and Monroe Beardsley. "The Concept of Meter: An Exercise in Abstraction." *PMLA* 54 (1959); rpt. in Chatman, Seymour, and Samuel R. Levin, eds. *Essays on the Language of Literature.* Boston: Houghton Mifflin, 1967. 91-114.

Three: Chaucer's Regular Iambic Pentameter Lines

The title of this chapter is presumptuous. It assumes that Chaucer wrote in a regular meter. Unless one makes this assumption, however, it will be impossible to discover what Chaucer was doing when he wrote his poetry. As we said in the last chapter, scansion is in some ways a circular process. We assume that a poet was thinking of a particular pattern, and our job is to discover that pattern and understand how the poet worked with it. The problem with complete reliance on this assumption is that some people have a tendency to take a general rule and then apply it with bullheaded insistence. Unfortunately, there are very few rules in human experience which always work. We can be thankful that poets have had the good sense to violate the rules that they themselves set up. The forbidden can be very sweet.

To keep us from becoming too fumble-fingered in our approach to the versification of one of England's greatest versifiers, it will be useful for us to examine lines with some detail. We will assume that the lines under question are examples of iambic pentameter; I am letting you know now that the lines treated in this chapter have been chosen because they clearly illustrate the problems under question. Although we do not really know how Chaucer's English was pronounced, we will proceed with the assumption that historical linguistics has something reasonable to tell us about Chaucer's English. In addition, we will assume that the reader has had an introduction to Chaucer's pronunciation from his textbook or a pronunciation guide (Cable 59-61, Finnie 21-25, Hempl, and Kökeritz). However, we will proceed inductively, making assumptions and announcing them along the way. We could proceed by imposing scansions with a few summary rules, but it is more important to learn *how* and *why* than merely *what*.

Let us begin with a pair of lines and see how our circle of logic works itself out. Here are two lines from the *General Prologue*:

Bifil that in that seson on a day,

In Southwerk at the Tabard as I lay (I 19-20)[1]

The first thing to notice is that the last syllables of the lines rhyme (*day*/*lay*). We can assume that the rhyme was intentional, especially when we look around the rest of the poem and see that other pairs of lines end with similar matchings of final syllables. This kind of observation may seem simple-minded, but simple-mindedness can sometimes be a virtue. In this case, our observation is very important: we will assume that since Chaucer took some pains to have the line ends rhyme, he held them in special aesthetic reverence. We assume that he gave special attention to rhyme and thus that he may have had to alter what he intended to say for the sake of rhyme. Further, we can assume that he may also have had to change the syntax of sentences so that the rhyme words came at the appropriate places in the lines. With this consideration, we can also assume that Chaucer may have intended to give his rhyme words special rhythmic prominence. This is a host of assumptions, but none of them asks too much of the reader—at least not yet. But I ask you then to consider the start of our scansion, prominence on the last syllable of each line:

/
Bifil that in that seson on a day,

/
In Southwerk at the Tabard as I lay

It will be useful to look first at the second line for clues about line structure. The first thing we can do is to look at the dissyllabic words. As we shall see, Chaucer's dissyllabic words are not always useful guides, but in this line they are helpful. The first dissyllabic word, *Southwerk,* is an apparent compound. Assuming that compounding worked in Chaucer's English the way that it works in ours, we can give stress to the first syllable of *Southwerk*. (We will not worry about the level of stress on the second element for a moment.) Knowing that we have a major stress on the first syllable of the compound, we can pair the first syllable of the line with it to make a foot. The preposition has less prominence than the following noun:

x / | /
In Southwerk at the Tabard as I lay

Proceeding with dissyllabic words, we can examine *Tabard*. Here our assignment is not quite as easy to make. As a two-syllable English word, we would put the stress

---

[1] Benson, Larry D. (Editor), THE RIVERSIDE CHAUCER, Third Edition. Copyright © 1987 by Houghton Mifflin Company. Used with permission.

on the first syllable of *Tabard*—but the word is French in origin. As we shall see, some words which have stress on first syllables for us often have stress on other syllables for Chaucer because the words were only recently borrowed from French and still retained French pronunciation patterns. Seeing no other reason not to do so at this time, we will assume that the name of this inn is to be pronounced as a nativized word with stress on the first syllable. Leaving aside the second syllable for a moment, we can place the stressed syllable of the noun next to its article and see another foot:

```
x   /  |     |  x  /|          /
In Southwerk at the Tabard as I lay
```

The observant student will have noticed that the syllables of this line are now lining up into fairly obvious groups of twos. We can easily etch out another foot. We gave *lay* prominence for rhyme, but we can also promote it for grammatical reasons. The reader will remember that in chapter one we intuitively assigned relative weights to grammatical categories. Here we have a pronoun and a verb. Although different contexts will provide different solutions, in this context we can see the verb gaining more prominence than the pronoun. With this observation, we add another foot to the scansion of the line:

```
x   /  |     |  x  /|       |x  /
In Southwerk at the Tabard as I lay
```

Now we run into some trouble. *Southwerk,* we decided, is a compound noun. Normally, we then expect the second element to carry secondary stress. However, I will argue here that it does not. *Southwerk*, while a compound noun, is also a place name. A peculiar feature of proper names, especially place names, is that they often lose their literal meaning and become merely significations for specific places. As such, the names often undergo great changes. A really aberrant example is a name like *Worcester*. According to historical linguistics, we can assume that the name at one time had three pronounced syllables. However, today the inhabitants of this place (one in England and one in Massachusetts) pronounce the name with two syllables (as if it were spelled *Wooster).* You are probably already familiar with this reduction in the term *Worcestershire sauce*, pronounced commonly as if it were spelled *Woostershir sauce.* Thus, it is not too difficult to believe that *Southwerk* (like modern *Norfolk)* may have been pronounced at one time with a heavy secondary stress on the second syllable, but that as Chaucer heard it, the secondary stress had been completely reduced. In fact, the element may have lost all of its semantic force, a situation that would render reduction even more arguable. In this case, we could claim that the following preposition in a fully pronounced form would get more prominence than the last syllable of *Southwerk*. In such a case, we can add another foot:

x /   I x /I x /I   Ix /
In Southwerk at the Tabard as I lay

We are then left with only one foot to account for. Here we are also on shaky grounds if we worry about the French pronunciation of *Tabard*, but as the name of an inn owned by the down-to-earth Host, we can give it the English pronunciation. In addition, since the second element has no independent semantic force for Middle English speakers, it has less prominence than it could have. In this case, the subordinating conjunction gains more prominence, and we proudly hail a completely scanned line of iambic pentameter:

x /   I x /I x /I x /Ix /
In Southwerk at the Tabard as I lay

Our accomplishment is held together with a web of assumptions, many of them tenuous. Perhaps we could find an easier line to start with, but this line gives us a sense of the kinds of problems one may encounter when scanning Chaucer. However, what is important here is that although we came up with a standard iambic pentameter line, we did not automatically force the pattern on the line. We examined each part of the line to find ways of justifying the application of the pattern. The result, while indeed tenuous, is not phonologically offensive—as long as the reader does not try to force all the stresses to the same heights and all the unstresses to the same depths.

The first line of the pair we have chosen presents different challenges to the scanner. Starting with dissyllabic words, we examine *Bifil* and *seson*. *Bifil* is the easier of the two to reckon with. Its Modern English equivalent is *befell*, a verb with stress on the second syllable. This verb follows the Germanic pattern of stressing verbs on the root syllable. The first syllable of both the Middle English form and the Modern English form is a verbal prefix; the second syllable is the root. This verb follows the pattern we also see in *become, beset, bedeck*, and others. Thus we have a ready-made foot at the beginning of the line:

x /I   /
Bifil that in that seson on a day,

The second dissyllabic word *seson* looks easy on the surface, but in actuality it is somewhat of a problem. It is a word of Romance origin and can have stress on the second element in Chaucer's English. Here, however, we will assume that it has been Anglicized and receives stress on the first syllable. The word, of course, corresponds to the Modern English word *season*, which has stress on the first syllable. If we then compare the stressed syllable of *seson* with the stress likely to be placed on the demonstrative article *that*, we see another foot emerge:

```
x / |     | x  /|         /
```
Bifil that in that seson on a day,

An easy foot to complete next is the last one. It offers an article before a noun with rhyme prominence:

```
x / |     | x  /|      | x /
```
Bifil that in that seson on a day,

This leaves two feet that are easily resolved. In the second foot, we see a subordinating conjunction and a preposition. Grammar is not much of a clue here, but syllabic burden, especially in terms of length, makes *in* seem more weighted than *that*. In the fourth foot, we have two syllables that are spelled with the same letters. One is the unstressed second syllable of a word we analyzed above, and the other is a preposition. Although I admit that such judgments are weakly supported, I think that it may not be too ludicrous to say that based on the patterns of Modern English, the second syllable of *seson* may get a reduced vowel while the vowel of *on* may well be a fully articulated open *o*. In this case, the iamb is readily apparent. If the reader fails to grant these arguments, I resort to the expectation caused by the meter: as we read along, we get into a pattern, and the pattern easily promotes the second syllable in each foot and demotes the first. Such is the nature of rhythm, even atemporal rhythm (cf. *tick-tick* = *tick-tock*). Our line ends up looking like this:

```
x / |  x  /|  x  /|x  / |x /
```
Bifil that in that seson on a day,

This is how far one can go on a few assumptions.

   Sometimes, however, our assumptions can get us into a crux. For example, our assumption that rhyming syllables gain prominence can make us admit that other givens in our thinking need to be modified. As speakers of a language that has suffered from a couple of centuries of linguistic legislation, we normally assume that there is just one way of doing something like pronouncing a word. Many of our dictionaries will give alternate pronunciations, but most people seem skeptical of such liberalism. However, when we read Chaucer, we need to look at his language with a keener appreciation of variation. From our standpoint, we can say that Chaucer's language was in flux, but Chaucer did not share our historical perspective. From his point of view, his language offered variety. Alternate pronunciations were available to him for words, and he used the variations to suit his purposes (Burnley and Eliason). Centuries later, in some cases, one or other of the variants won out as the "standard" form, but to force such a standard on Chaucer is anachronistic and silly. The English of Chaucer's day was a language new in social importance. It had been the language of only lower-class people in the centuries preceding Chaucer's, and its speakers were enjoying a new prestige. In addition, Chaucer's London was an exciting place with an influx of people from all over England, and these people came with varieties of English that were often mutually unintelligible. To confuse matters further, it was still fashionable for Englishmen to learn French, and people around Chaucer probably spoke French with varying degrees of proficiency. English speakers were using a great many French words, and with the varying influence that French had on all these English speakers, we can see that it is possible for certain words to have a variety of pronunciations—some more like the French original, others fully or partially Anglicized. Indeed, these kinds of variations became the lament of stodgy Englishmen for the next four hundred years. The attitude survives at any meeting of English teachers.

This kind of variety has certain implications for the scansion of Chaucer's poetry. Some of these implications will be treated in detail in the next chapter, but here we will be concerned with gross differences in stress assignments in both native and French words. Let's start with a native word first, *comyng*. We will disregard for the moment that the word also has a form with a final -*e*, a more fitting subject for the next chapter. Normally, the word appears to be accented on the first syllable as it should be according to the rules of English word formation: root syllables get stress over suffixes. That's the rule, plain and simple. However, Chaucer is not above placing the suffix in the last stressed position in the line:

Whan that he cam, som manere honest thyng,

For which they were as glad of his comyng (VII 49-50)

As we mentioned above, our assumption about rhyme can get us into a fix, and here is an example of one of those places. It is fairly obvious that Chaucer intended to rhyme *thyng* with the last syllable of *comyng*. In that case, we assume that he wanted to stress -*yng* over *com*-. If we assume this, we fly up in the face of our verb formation rule; but if we do not assume it, we end up with a very peculiar poetic effect. A recent writer has opted for this peculiar effect in order to save these kinds of assumptions about linguistic stress (Robinson). But I say that it would be wise to junk the rule in this case. In Middle English, there were competing forms of the present participle and gerund ending; they appear as -*ende* or -*ande* and become the Modern English ending spelled in informal written English as -*in'* (i. e., *comin'*: "She'll be *comin'* 'roun' the mountain when she comes."). With this kind of variation to be heard, it is easy to imagine speakers favoring one form or another and feeling a need to give some kind of prominence or other to the ending. In addition, it is also easy to imagine that there were speakers upon whom the influence of French was great (that is, they spoke French first and English second) and for whom the English verb formation rule did not work. We can argue then that Chaucer, who hobnobbed with aristocrats (those most likely to speak French), simply had enough experience with hearing English pronounced with a heavy French accent that stressing the second syllable did not seem out of the ordinary.

This argument is not too outrageous: I have relatives who work with Chicano laborers, and these relatives often imitate the pronunciation of Chicano English. What started off as a joke, however, has become a more or less "normal" way of talking for them. If one of these relatives were a poet, he might be inclined to write verse and utilize a Chicano pronunciation. He would be thought clever by his peers. The moral of the story is that Chaucer may also be thought clever for using such variations. Chaucer seems to be one of the most careful versifiers in English, and we even have records of his complaining to his scrivener about the text of his work. Rather than having Chaucer reversing a foot at the end of the line and losing the effect of the rhyme he so carefully put together and rather than saying that Chaucer is just a sloppy poet who runs roughshod over the English language, we might just say that there is reason to suspect that *-yng* could receive stress in varieties of English that Chaucer heard and that when Chaucer needed one of these varietal forms to finish a line, he used it. The form neither offended his ear nor the ears of his contemporaries. They did not have the cursed luxuries of the dictionary and the grammar book.

Words of French origin present similar kinds of problems. Above we noted that *seson* was such a word. This word is apparently usually accented on the first syllable. My evidence for this is the relatively few incidences of this word as a rhyme word in Chaucer. The word generally appears within a line where it apparently has stress on the first syllable, much as it does in the line discussed above. However, there is a case where our assumption about promotion for rhyme argues for stress on the last syllable:

To ech of hem his tyme and his seson, (V 1034)

The second syllable of the word is the rhyming syllable for the line, and *seson* is meant to rhyme with *declinacion*. A student who wants to know how to scan the words in each case should do two things: one, thoroughly examine the line in question for other clues of the line's structure; two, consult the Chaucer concordance (Tatlock and Kennedy) to see how the word operates elsewhere in Chaucer's verse.

Following this plan, we can see that *honour,* another French borrowing, behaves in a different fashion. This word generally has its main stress on the second syllable: it usually comes at line-end in Chaucer and thus falls prey to our assumption about rhyme promotion. Here is an example in context:

      x / l x   /   l x   /   l x   / l x /
    He festeth hem, and dooth so greet labour

```
   x /l x   /   lx    /   l x  /l x  /
```
To esen hem and doon hem al honour (I 2193-94)

Since so many examples of this word fall at line-end, it is difficult to find counter-examples this early in our exposition. But one does appear in *The Shipman's Tale*:

```
   x  /   l x  / l x  /l x  /   l x  /
```
To doon therwith myn honour and my prow, (VII 408)

To scan the line otherwise mocks simplicity, and we get a line with two reversed feet (a subject for a later chapter):

```
   x  /   l x  / l  /  xl /  x l  x  /
```
To doon therwith myn honour and my prow,

Although I will admit that a poet could do such a thing, it hardly seems likely that Chaucer has done so here. This scansion offers us two reversed feet in a row without any reasonable motivation. The solution is to realize that Chaucer had two pronunciations of *honour* to choose from, one still French in nature and the other Englished.

This chapter is short, but it is short for a good reason. We have looked at rather easy lines and have avoided ones with the troublesome problems that have beset Chaucerian scholars. We have avoided these problems so that we could look at Chaucer in his simplest form, for I believe that until we can scan these "easy" lines we will only compound our confusion by tackling more difficult issues. A smart-aleck may remark that such an approach obscures the reality of Chaucer's verse, but I will arrogantly add that it sharpens our vision of Chaucer's verse. We simply must know what we are looking for before we can find it.

Exercise 3.1

1. What effect does rhyme have on stress assignment?
2. What arguments can be given for promoting rhymed syllables?
3. Why might there be pronunciation variants in Chaucer's English?
4. How should we regard Chaucer's use of these variants?
5. Try to find examples of Modern English verse in which poets use dialectal or archaic variants. Justify the use where you find it. For example, make a collection of poems that use the word *bough*. Do you or any of your friends use the word? Where is the word found?

Exercise 3.2

Directions: Scan the following lines from *The Miller's Tale*. Identify problems in the scansion. Discuss the problems and their solutions.

1. "Therof," quod Absolon, "be as be may. (I 3783)
2. This carpenter goth doun, and comth ageyn, (I 3496)
3. Hir forheed shoon as bright as any day, (I 3310)
4. And of his craft he was a carpenter. (I 3189)
5. This parissh clerk, this joly Absolon, (I 3348)
6. And thus lith Alison and Nicholas, (I 3653)
7. In ronnen for to gauren on this man, (I 3827)
8. "Allas," quod Absolon, "and weylawey, (I 3714)
9. And Absolon, hym fil no bet ne wers, (I 3733)
10. This Nicholas anon leet fle a fart
    As greet as it had been a thonder-dent,
    That with the strook he was almoost yblent;
    And he was redy with his iren hoot, (I 3806-09)
11. And therwith spak this clerk, this Absolon, (I 3804)
12. "Of this despit awroken for to be. (I 3752)

References and Suggested Reading

Benson, Larry D., ed. *The Riverside Chaucer*. 3rd ed. Boston: Houghton Mifflin, 1987.

Burnley, David. "Linguistic Diversity." In *A Guide to Chaucer's Language*. Norman: Univ. of Oklahoma Press, 1983. 108-32.

Cable, Thomas. *A Companion to Baugh and Cable's History of the English Language*. Englewood Cliffs: Prentice-Hall, 1983.

Eliason, Norman E. "The Sound of the Verse." In *The Language of Chaucer's Poetry: An Appraisal of the Verse, Style, and Structure*. Anglistica, 18. Copenhagen: Rosenkilde and Bagger, 1972. 16-59.

Finnie, W. Bruce. *The Stages of English: Texts, Transcriptions, Exercises*. New York: Houghton Mifflin, 1972.

Hempl, George. *Chaucer's Pronunciation and the Spelling of the Ellesmere MS*. 1893; rpt. Norwood, Pa.: Norwood Editions, 1978.

Kökeritz, Helge. *A Guide to Chaucer's Pronunciation*. 1961; rpt. Toronto: Univ. of Toronto Press, 1978.

Robinson, Ian. *Chaucer's Prosody: A Study of the Middle English Verse Tradition.* Cambridge: Cambridge Univ. Press, 1971.

Tatlock, John S. P., and A. G. Kennedy. *Concordance to the Complete Works of Geoffrey Chaucer and to the Romaunt of the Rose.* 1927; rpt. Gloucester, Mass.: Peter Smith, 1963.

Four: The Syllables That Count

If the lines offered as examples in the last chapter were typical of Chaucer's poetry, our job as prosodists would be very simple. Unfortunately, such is not the case. Not quite two hundred years after Chaucer died, his verse was misunderstood. The best opinion had it that Chaucer was a very sloppy metrist. Spenser, for example, read Chaucer's iambic pentameter as a kind of loose tetrameter. Things got so dismal that both Dryden and Pope felt that they had to polish up Chaucer to make him acceptable to their contemporaries. All of this misunderstanding developed from the changes that occurred in the English language in the century or so after Chaucer died, and indeed it has been suggested that many of the changes were already taking place in Chaucer's time and that Chaucer just happened to be conservative in his use of English. Whatever the case, it is obvious that in the next century English underwent massive changes in pronunciation. This is the time of the Great Vowel Shift, a process that shifted "long" vowels so that written English vowels are no longer pronounced with their usual continental values. In addition, a much more important change took place as far as scansion is concerned: many unaccented *e*'s were lost from pronunciation.

Not all authorities are in agreement over what happened in this latter case or when it happened (Southworth *vs.* Donaldson; cf. other references). However, it is important to look in some detail at the *e*'s in Chaucer's English, for without some acknowledgement of these unaccented *e*'s, Chaucer's verse just does not scan very well. Accepting the existence of these *e*'s is somewhat a matter of faith, and we must admit that sometimes the faith has been too dogmatic. Because of this dogmatism, we have had to suffer from heretics who are often frightening in the strength of their adherence to their own errors. We forgive them and ask them to return to the faith. We admonish the dogmatic pronouncements of scholars from Tyrwhitt to Ten Brink, but we accept their faith in the structural integrity of Chaucer's verse, based as it is on firm belief in the slippery *e* and its vital importance to the shape of Chaucer's lines.

The importance of the *e*, however, is only part of the more general concern of this chapter. Foot-prosody demands that there be only a certain number of syllables in a line. By and large, the number of syllables in Chaucer's lines is relatively stable. In very many cases, the lines have what appears to be an extra syllable, and sometimes the lines seem to fall short in number. Because of this variable situation, scanning Chaucer can sometimes get difficult. Here we need to use our wits to draw on historical linguistics, common sense, and practical aesthetics to make Chaucer's verse work.

It is probably very useful to start this discussion with practical examples. I offer the following lines as examples of "regular" lines of iambic pentameter, regular only if you know how to fiddle with Chaucer's *e*'s:

> For which this millere stal bothe mele and corn

> An hundred tyme moore than biforn; (I 3995-96)

If we give a verbatim translation of the lines into Modern English, we get the following:

> For which the miller stole both meal and corn

> A hundred times more than before

Although such a translation is metrically deficient, it does provide us with some useful information. We can scan the translation in this fashion:

```
    x   / |  x   / |x  / |  x    / |x    /
For which this miller stole both meal and corn

x  / |  x   /  |  /   x |  x /
A hundred times more than before.
```

There are a couple of observations we should make: One, in Modern English we pronounce some of the written *e*'s but not all of them. The ones that we pronounce, at least here, are parts of morphological structures even if the morphemes of which they are a part are fossils like *-red*. Two, we do not come out with a very regular scansion. The second line has only four feet, and there also seems to be a reversed foot, something we have not talked about yet in any detail.

If Chaucer's lines have as many syllables as the Modern English equivalent, we have to change either our conception of Chaucer as a versifier or our conception of Chaucer's intended meter. We make our decision on the basis of taste and instinct, and we conclude that Chaucer was a good versifier (it seems incongruous that such a good storyteller could be such a lousy versifier when any pathetic hack seems to be able to make up lines of even meters) and that Chaucer's meter here is iambic pentameter. Our conclusions, of course, are assumptions, and the power of observation that we are born with leads us to suspect that something else must be happening in Chaucer's language to support our view of his talents and our prejudice for regular iambic pentameter lines. What we turn to is the *e*.

If we suspend our objections to the method for a moment, we can scan the lines as follows and get the lines we want. Holding our noses as we plunge in, we can come up with the following scansion:

```
    x    /  |  x   / |x    / |  x    /  |x    /
    For which this millere stal bothe mele and corn
```

```
    x   /  |x   /| x  / |x  /  | x/
    An hundred tyme moore than biforn;
```

The careful reader will have noticed that some of the unaccented *e*'s have been counted in the metrical scheme, but that others have not. The simplest explanation for the inclusion of some *e*'s and the exclusion of others is that they are used when they are needed. However, we can devise additional explanations to support this claim. Some of the unused *e*'s can have their exclusion justified on phonological grounds. The *e* in *mele* is followed by another vowel, the *a* of *and*. We can justify this exclusion in two ways. One, the *e* and the *a* are somehow pronounced as one syllable—as in a diphthong. Or two, the *e* is merely elided before the following vowel, Middle English then having a phonological rule which avoids placing an unaccented *e* of whatever phonological value before another unstressed vowel. The case of *millere* is somewhat different: here we see the influence of a liquid, in this case *r*. In the presence of such a liquid, it is common to see one of the two *e*'s as elidible. The last example in this line, *bothe*, is different yet again. Here the "first" syllable is demoted; if the word were spoken in isolation as two syllables, the second syllable would be less stressed than the first syllable. It would not be too outrageous to say that when the first syllable is demoted in the context of a line, the second syllable then suffers some further demotion—in this case it is dropped.

The second line provides examples for understanding when to pronounce the final *e*. The first word in the line with an unaccented *e*, *hundred*, is also a Modern English word, and thus we can assume that the vowel was also pronounced in Middle English. The next two words are problematic, however. Here *tyme* and *more* function as two-syllable words. We have two ways to justify their functioning in this way. One, they were in the mental lexicon of Middle English speakers as two-syllable words that could lose their final syllables when they were followed by vowels or placed in the environment of a liquid. Or two, these words were monosyllabic in the mental lexicon of the Middle English speaker and became dissyllabic only when the following word began with a consonant. An example of this kind of practice has been given in regard to Italians, say, who learn English and retain Italian prosody in their speech (Conner). They have a tendency to provide a vowel between the final consonant of one word and the beginning consonant of the next: "I'm*a* gonna buy you some-*a* pizza." Such could very well have been the practice of Middle English speakers, and our study of Chaucer's verse points to this practice as possible.

The reader may now be very well confused by this discussion and may need some explanation of the origin of this final unaccented *e*. Sometimes, the final unaccented *e* is *organic* and represents the remnants of the Old English inflectional system; at other times, the final unaccented *e* is *inorganic* and has appeared because of analogy. The organic *e* then is an inflection, an affix that signals the grammatical function of a word. For example, an *s* or an *es* at the end of a word in Modern English may signal that the word is a plural noun or a third person singular present tense indicative verb. An *ed* attached to a word signals that it is a verb in the past tense. Old English had a very extensive system of inflectional endings. These endings provided the Old English speaker with a variety of information about things such as number, tense, person, gender, or case. While Modern English relies to a great extent on word order to show relationships between words, Old English relied on word endings to signal the same kinds of relationships. Word order was not free in Old English by any means, but it was of minor importance in telling who did what to whom. Without getting too far afield, we can note that in Modern English there is a great difference between the sentence *The dog bit the cat* and the sentence *The cat bit the dog*. In Old English, word endings and articles would determine what did the biting and what got bitten.

An example from Old English will help to illustrate the extent of its inflectional system. Here is a sentence from *The Harrowing of Hell*:

> Ac sē wuldorfæsta Cyning and ūre heofenlīca Hlāford þā nolde þǣra
> dēofla ġemāðeles nā māre habban. (Moore and Knott 203)

> [But then the wonderous King and our heavenly Lord would no longer
> tolerate the speeches of the devils.]

The article *se* indicates that the noun *Cyning* is the subject, and here we actually have a twice-named singular subject similar in structure to Modern English phrases like *The winner and new champion is Aldo Bosco*. The adjectives *wuldorfæsta* and *heofenlīca* both end in the weak adjectival ending appropriate for singular masculine nominative nouns. The article and noun combination *þǣra dēofla* is inflected as a possessive plural. *ġemāðeles* is inflected for the accusative plural. *māre* ends in the typical adverbial ending. *habban* [Modern English *have*] is inflected as an infinitive.

As you can see, the Old English speaker had a great number of grammatical endings to work with. This sentence only scratches the surface, however, of the inflectional possibilities in Old English.

These and other inflectional endings were reduced considerably, however, between the times of Old English and Chaucer's Middle English. Scholars are not entirely sure about how this process took place, but someway or another two processes seem to have occurred at the same time. In late Old English, unaccented vowels were reduced to a schwa. The vowels *a, u, o, i,* and *e* had been used to signal grammatical differences between words in Old English, but after all of these unaccented vowels were reduced to schwa, endings no longer indicated many grammatical distinctions. At some point in the process, word order took over the function of determining grammatical relationships. However, the schwas, written as *e*'s, survived—and they survived in many cases despite the lack of grammatical information in the sound. In Chaucer's English, the unaccented *e*—whether final or internal—still often retained some recognizable grammatical information. The *e* seems to have been pronounced on most weak adjectives (adjectives preceded by articles or personal pronouns); on verbs inflected for person or tense (although verbal endings with two *e*'s probably lost one); on many nouns inflected for plural number or the possessive; and on adverbs.

However, simple phonological change does not explain much of what happened. Sometimes *e*'s argued by linguistic history (organic *e*'s) were not pronounced; sometimes *e*'s not justified by linguistic history (inorganic *e*'s) were pronounced. These anomalies can be accounted for by two processes: words received *e*'s through analogy with words that had them for historical reasons; then, with there being no grammatical structure at stake, the pronunciation of the *e*'s became merely a function of stress-timing. Apparently, there was some confusion in Chaucer's day about which *e*'s to pronounce and which not to pronounce, but such confusion allowed Chaucer great metrical flexibility. Anyone who has tried to write English meters knows how useful it would be to have a choice of words with monosyllabic or dissyllabic forms. We grant Chaucer that choice, and we reap the benefits. This option allowed Chaucer to write verse in an easy colloquial style, and the additional syllables on words that are otherwise just like ours make them quaint and musical to us. Soon after Chaucer's time, the final unaccented *e* disappeared, but in Chaucer's day the *e* was a phonological variant that Chaucer could employ as he saw fit.

Without granting Chaucer this liberty—or the facts of his tongue—many lines in Chaucer will not scan according to the iambic-pentameter scheme. If we approach the following line with ears attuned only to major stresses, we get a very lame line indeed:

/   /   /
He rometh to the carpenteres hous, (I 3694)

Our line is not much better if we find some prominence in the preposition. Then we get a line of only four stresses, a possible scansion for some readers to be sure, but a scansion that abandons the too recurrent pattern of five stresses in Chaucer's poetry:

>   x /   x   /   x /   x x   /
>   He rometh to the carpenteres hous,

As in all things in prosody, taste and good sense are the deciding criteria, and if we decide that our Chaucer writes in a regular meter, then with a few sound assumptions we can scan his lines with this pattern. In this case, we scan the line in question with five feet:

>   x /l x   /l x /l x /lx /
>   He rometh to the carpenteres hous,

This scansion assumes that the verbal inflection -eth can be pronounced, and later poetry seems to indicate that it can be. This scansion also assumes that the preposition can be accented in a foot, and when we compare the inflectional syllable to the preposition, the preposition wins out. Further, the scansion assumes that *carpenteres* in this instance has four syllables. The word has three in Modern English, but even in Modern English it is a phonologically conditioned but common thing for the possessive to be pronounced (*Mr. Fish's house*). We grant that in Modern English an /r/ does not condition a syllabic pronunciation for the possessive, but this exclusion in Modern English does not apply in Chaucer's English.

We can thus establish a method for dealing with Chaucer's slippery lines. Here is a line with a number of *e*'s, some of which are pronounced:

>   With scalled browes blake and piled berd. (I 627)

The first thing to do normally in scanning a line of verse is to examine the rhyme syllable. Here the rhyme is on the *-erd* of *berd*. We give stress to this syllable right away. Then we approach the multisyllabic words. Here, however, is where our process comes to a screeching halt. We have four words in the line that may have two syllables: *scalled, browes, blake*, and *piled*. If we counted all of the *e*'s, the line would have too many syllables, so what we must do is eliminate one of the *e*'s. We do this by grouping syllables into iambic feet that do not require us to use the unaccented *e*'s. This process immediately places together *With scall-* and *and pi-*. In these cases we have function words placed before adjectival past participles. Our stress assignments then are easy to make:

```
    x   / |                lx    /|    /
```
With scalled browes blake and piled berd.

Marked out like this, the line then becomes easier to deal with. It becomes obvious that the last foot will have to include the *-ed* of *piled* if the line is not to be defective. The second thing that these first assignments of stress show us is that *blake* probably does not have its *e* pronounced. There are two reasons for this: the *e* precedes a vowel, and the vowel is unaccented. In this case, the *e* does not count in either pronunciation or scansion. If this *e* is eliminated, the other two *e*'s in question can be pronounced and can figure in the scansion. When the inflectional syllables are then weighed against the stress of the syllables of the following noun and adjective, there is no question about the stress assignments:

```
    x   / | x    /| x    / | x    /|x    /
```
With scalled browes blake and piled berd.

By a process of elimination, we have established the scansion of this line. With a little practice, however, such scanning can become automatic. One can get a feel for how the lines work. At this point, however, hearing the line becomes easier than justifying how one arrives at the scansion.

So far we have not asked the reader to accept too much on faith. We have made a few assumptions based on our experience with the English language as we speak it and as we know it to have been in Chaucer's day. We have made aesthetic judgments, but we have been able to come back in the circle of metrical logic to justify our initial assumptions. At any rate, we have closed the circle. We now come to a discussion that requires faith for understanding and shared taste for that faith. Here is the dogma: Unaccented *e*'s at the end of the line in Chaucer are always pronounced.

Some justifications for this belief can be gathered. The first is that the best manuscripts of Chaucer's poetry have couplets rhyming combinations of stressed syllables and following *e*'s. Such a matching is called feminine rhyme. Even though some cases of these lines are doubtful, there are cases where it is obvious that Chaucer meant to have feminine rhyme:

```
    x   /    | x  /| x    /| x /    lx   /| x
```
That streight was comen fro the court of Rome.

```
    x /    | x /    | x    /|x    /| x / | x
```
Ful loude he soong "Com hider, love, to me!" (I 671-72)

This example is often cited as evidence of Chaucer's use of a feminine rhyme that relies on the pronunciation of the final unaccented *e*. I believe that it is an acceptable example of the claim, but there is an argument against the scansion with an eleventh syllable. If we grant, say, that Chaucer uses the *e* only to separate stresses, then we have no reason to sound the final *e* in the first line. If the opposition says that *Rome* has to rhyme with *to me*, we could answer that the last two words could be reduced to one syllable with the final *e* left unpronounced. If the opposition says that such a claim is ridiculous, we could answer that Chaucer is making a joke. However, such a pronunciation for *to me* is very un-English. If we then agreed that such a pronunciation would be un-English, we could still argue that *Rome* is very obviously the name of an Italian city whose name is pronounced with two syllables (*Roma*). We could say that although the normal pronunciation for Chaucer would make the word one syllable, in this case he is making a joke about the Pardoner's *savoire faire* with the pronunciation of the name of the Holy City. So much for the good example. Faith is still required to see the feminine rhyme in general.

Other examples of feminine rhyme can be found. Here is one that can make sense to someone who speaks Modern English:

  x / |x / | x / | x / | x / | x
  For hooly chirches good moot been despended

  x / |x / | x / | x x / | x / | x
  On hooly chirches blood, that is descended. (I 3983-84)

In these lines we have nothing particularly alien to worry about. The unaccented *e*'s are part of inflectional endings that we pronounce in Modern English on the basis of phonological rules. The example, however, does not really advance our argument very far. Since we pronounce these *e*'s in Modern English, they do not tell us much about *e*'s in Middle English that we do not pronounce in Modern English. But these lines do show us that feminine rhymes are possible in Chaucer's verse.

If we take the last set of lines together with the first we examined for the presence of feminine rhymes, we can organize our argument in two steps before asking the reader to get the gift of grace. The last lines show the possibility of feminine rhyme. The first set shows how a final unaccented *e* (that is not pronounced in Modern English) can figure into the scheme of a feminine rhyme. The next step is to accept the feminine rhyme in lines like the following:

  x / |x / | x / |x / | x / | x
  And Alisoun ful softe adoun she spedde;

  x / |x / | x /| x / |x / | x
  Withouten wordes mo they goon to bedde, (I 3649-50)

To accept these hypermetrical syllables, we have to make a few assumptions. One, we could say (with some circularity, of course) that Chaucer was fond of feminine rhymes, and if we push the point about the line-final unaccented *e*, we can say that he had an overwhelming fondness for feminine rhyme (Buck and Malone). Two, we could say that the final *e* in Chaucer is generally pronounced and that it is suppressed only in certain environments. Earlier we hedged on what the process was: either suppression of *e*'s or promotion of *e*'s for syllable-timing purposes. Three, we could say that the final *e* could be either pronounced or not pronounced in Chaucer's English and that Chaucer probably pronounced it within the line to separate clashing stresses. He pronounced it at the end of lines to mark their ends. Further, we can conclude that Chaucer just plain liked feminine rhymes with *e* and that we should grant him that like and see the *e*'s where provided by the manuscripts and add them where they are lacking for one reason or another in the manuscripts. However, I do not believe that we can force the point. It is not unreasonable to insist that intralineal final unaccented *e*'s must be pronounced to provide the unstressed members of feet. But it may become unreasonable to insist that line-final *e*'s be pronounced. The results of counting these hypermetric syllables, however, are delightful. The verse that emerges is line- and rhyme-conscious. It tends to slow down at line end and to mark rhyme. Marked rhyme in syntactically complex narrative makes sheer delight arise from form.

If the reader grants the pronunciation of the *e*'s in the last examples, then he will easily grant the same for *e*'s that follow vowels in the last stressed position in the line:

      x / |x   / |x   / | x   / |x /|x
      Do wey youre handes, for youre curteisye!"

      x   /| x/ | x   /| x / | x /|x
      This Nicholas gan mercy for to crye, (I 3287-88)

If one gets squeamish about these kinds of lines because of the hiatus that may occur between these two sounds, we can point out that what we may have here is a semivowel between two vowels /ijə/.

There are other problems with counting syllables that will be treated in the next chapter. This chapter has dealt primarily with Chaucer's troublesome *e*. We cannot claim to have resolved all of the difficulties, but we have presented the arguments on both sides. In short, our scansion of the *e* becomes an aesthetic decision based on our assumptions about the nature of Chaucer's meter and his language. We assume that he is writing a regular meter and that he had phonological variants to choose from. Further, the phonological variants are the results of the collapse of the Old English inflectional system and the process of analogy operating in the resulting confusion. Appreciation of this confusion may be difficult for us to summon, but despite our insistence on linguistic unity, we ourselves participate in much more linguistic variation than we often want to admit. Chaucer did not study English grammar as devised by eighteenth-century prescriptivists. He was probably much more comfortable with his language than we are with ours. He was not its slave; he was its master. Our knowing when to scan his final unaccented *e*'s leads us to an appreciation of his mastery.

Exercise 4.1

Directions: Scan the following lines. Justify your decisions on which unaccented *e*'s to include in your scansion.

1. Inspired hath in every holt and heeth (I 6)
2. His hors were goode, but he was nat gay. (I 74)
3. That fro the tyme that he first bigan (I 44)
4. That I was of hir felaweshipe anon, (I 32)
5. For thogh a wydwe hadde noght a sho, (I 253)
6. He was the beste beggere in his hous; (I 252)
7. His bootes clasped faire and fetisly. (I 273)
8. Stood redy covered al the longe day. (I 354)
9. Of fees and robes hadde he many oon. (I 317)

Exercise 4.2

Directions: Scan the following lines. Discuss reasons in each case that could be given for justifying the hypermetricity of each pair.

1. But al be that he was a philosophre,
   Yet hadde he but litel gold in cofre; (I 297-98)
2. For catel hadde they ynogh and rente,
   And eek hir wyves wolde it wel assente; (I 373-74)
3. For ech of hem made oother for to wynne—
   Hir frendshipe nas nat newe to bigynne. (I 427-28)
4. And swich he was ypreved ofte sithes.
   Ful looth were hym to cursen for his tithes, (I 485-86)
5. Whan that we come agayn fro Caunterbury.
   And for to make yow the moore mury, (I 801-02)
6. Where that ther kneled in the heighe weye
   A compaignye of ladyes, tweye and tweye, (I 897-98)

References and Suggested Reading

Babcock, Charlotte F. "A Study of the Metrical Use of the Inflectional *E* in Middle English, with Particular Reference to Chaucer and Lydgate." *PMLA* 29 (1914): 59-92.

Buck, Howard. "Chaucer's Use of Feminine Rhyme." *Modern Philology* 26 (1928): 13-14.

Child, F. J. "Observations on the Language of Chaucer and Gower." In Alexander J. Ellis. *On Early English Pronunciation with Special Reference to Shakspeare and Chaucer.* Part I. London: Trübner, 1869. 342-97.

Conner, Jack. *English Prosody from Chaucer to Wyatt.* Janua Linguarum, Series Practica, 193. The Hague: Mouton, 1974.

Donaldson, E. Talbot. "Chaucer's Final -*E*." *PMLA* 63 (1948): 1101-24.

Eliason, Norman E. "The Sound of the Verse." In *The Language of Chaucer's Poetry: An Appraisal of the Verse, Style, and Structure.* Anglistica, 18. Copenhagen: Rosenkilde and Bagger, 1972. 16-59.

Frankis, P. J. "The Syllabic Value of Final '-es' in English Versification about 1500." *Notes and Queries* 212 (1967): 11-12.

Kittredge, George Lyman. *Observations on the Language of Chaucer's Troilus.* Chaucer Society Publications, Series II, No. 28. London: Kegan Paul, Trench, Trübner and Co., 1891. 346-421.

Malone, Kemp. "Chaucer's Double Consonants and the Final *E*." *Mediaeval Studies* 18 (1956): 204-07.

McJimsey, Ruth B. *Chaucer's Irregular -E: A Demonstration Among Monosyllabic Nouns of the Exceptions to Grammatical and Metrical Harmony.* Diss. Columbia Univ. Morningside Heights, N. Y.: King's Crown Press, 1941.

Moore, Samuel, and Thomas A. Knott. *The Elements of Old English.* 10th ed. Rev. by James R. Hulbert. Ann Arbor: George Wahr, 1955.

Payne, Joseph. "The Use of the Final -*e* in Early English, and Especially in Chaucer's *Canterbury Tales.*" *Essays in Chaucer, His Life and Works.* Chaucer Society Publications, Series II, No. 9. London: Kegan Paul, Trench, Trübner, 1874; rpt. 1896. 83-154.

Robinson, Ian. *Chaucer's Prosody: A Study of the Middle English Verse Tradition.* Cambridge: Cambridge Univ. Press, 1971.

Samuels, M. L. "Chaucerian Final '-e.'" *Notes and Queries* 217 (1972): 445-48.

Skeat, Walter W. "An Essay on the Language and Versification of Chaucer." Part the Third, vii-xv. *The Poetical Works of Geoffrey Chaucer.* Ed. Richard Morris.

Rev. ed. London: Bell and Daldy, 1872. I, 172-96.

Southworth, James G. "Chaucer's Final -*E* (Continued)." *PMLA* 64 (1949), 601-09, 609-10.

—. "Chaucer's Final -*E* in Rhyme." *PMLA* 62 (1947): 910-35.

—. *The Prosody of Chaucer and His Followers: Supplementary Chapters to* Verses of Cadence. 1962; rpt. Westport, Conn.: Greenwood Press, 1978.

—. *Verses of Cadence: An Introduction to the Prosody of Chaucer and His Followers.* Oxford: Basil Blackwell, 1954.

Ten Brink, Bernhard. *The Language and Metre of Chaucer.* 2nd ed. Rev. by Friedrich Kluge. Trans. by M. Bentinck Smith. 1901; rpt. New York: Haskell House, 1968.

Topliff, Delores E. "Analysis of Singular Weak Adjective Inflection in Chaucer's Works." *Journal of English Linguistics* 4 (1970): 78-89.

Tyrwhitt, T. "Essay on the Language and Versification of Chaucer." In *The Poetical Works of Geoffrey Chaucer.* 1775; rpt. 1845; rpt. New York: AMS Press, 1972. 145-251.

Five: Some Basic Substitutions

Although we have already dealt with some rather complicated problems in line structure, we have treated only cases of lines made up of iambs. While it might be possible to write an acceptable long poem in lines of only iambs, such a poem would be unbearably dull and lifeless. *Gorboduc*, for example, a poetic drama of the sixteenth century, is often regarded as an example of a poem with a dull and lifeless meter because the poet failed to vary the rhythms in his lines of blank verse (unrhymed iambic pentameter). It is often said that rules are made to be broken, and the wisdom of this saw is applicable to versification. After hearing the same rhythm over and over again, we become entranced—if not hypnotized—and we doze off into daydreams interrupted only slightly by the text we are reading. We might say that some poets make special efforts to vary the rhythm of their verse to avoid putting us to sleep. But we may also say that perhaps some poets change the variety of their rhythms because they cannot make the words fit the meter. We might add that some poets probably do not give this aspect of meter much thought and that the pleasant surprises of rhythm that they present us are the products of their "good ears."

Shakespeare certainly had a good ear, and Chaucer had one too. While rhythm in Chaucer's verse will concern us in chapter seven, we can look at how Chaucer provides variation in his lines. Sometimes we have to admit that Chaucer varies his meter because he is just trying to make words fit in a syllable-counting scheme, but at other times he seems to be displaying a fine aesthetic sense. At any rate, Chaucer uses three different types of variation in foot structure. In what are often called substitutions, he will exchange iambs (x /) for trochees (/ x) or anapests (x x /). In addition, he often displays what we call headless lines.

A common substitution in Chaucer's verse is the trochaic substitution. Since the trochee changes the pattern of stress to stronger-weaker, this kind of substitution is often called a reversed foot. The most common place to find a trochaic substitution is in the first foot. This substitution is also found many times in the third foot. Occasionally, one may find a reversed second or fourth foot. The reversed fifth foot is a debatable subject and depends on one's sense of how rhyme promotion works. In many cases, the reversal may be debatable, but it is possible nonetheless to find lines that unequivocally contain reversed feet.

Here is an example of a line with a reversed first foot:

Milk and broun breed, in which she foond no lak, (VII 2844)

Final unaccented *e*'s do not foul us up in this line, and we can fairly easily see the reversal. Since we have no multisyllabic words in this line, we must turn to phrase structure to determine which syllables are stronger than others. Luckily, the line has ten obvious syllables, so we do not have to undergo any long process to get the syllable count right. The first clue to the foot structure may be found in the last two syllables. *lak* is the rhyme word, and it is preceded by a determiner. The last foot is thus determined, and it is an iamb:

```
                                          x  /
Milk and broun breed, in which she foond no lak,
```

Although we could work backward, it might be wise in this instance to look at the noun phrase *broun breed*. Here we have an adjective preceding a noun, and discounting that the locution may be a compound word, we can apply the nuclear stress rule to group the third and fourth syllables of the line into another iamb:

```
         |  x      /  |                   | x  /
Milk and broun breed, in which she foond no lak,
```

With this much established, we can work with the syllables lying between the established feet. The combination *she foond* is easy to scan—the preterite verb commands more burden than the personal pronoun. The remaining two syllables of *in which* offer no easy solution, but we can claim prominence for *which* over *in*. If we want, we can argue that the head word of the prepositional phrase, *which*, has more burden than the preposition. In this case, our scansion now looks like this:

```
         |  x      /  | x    /  |  x  /   | x  /
Milk and broun breed, in which she foond no lak,
```

We are left with the problem of what to do with the first foot, made obviously of the first two syllables, *Milk and*. Although there may be someone somewhere who might believe that prominence can be given to *and* because of some rhetorical purpose, I think that simple grammatical arguments here are much stronger. The noun has prominence over the conjunction because there is no indication that we should give some importance to the conjunction. With prominence given to the noun, we then have a reversed foot.

```
/   x
```
Milk and broun breed, in which she foond no lak,

As we said before, a reversed foot can provide relief from monotony, but the reversal is by no means jarring. In this instance, the reversal takes place at the beginning of the line, and the reader or the listener has really no way of knowing if the second element of the foot is going to be stronger or weaker than the first element until he hears it. In addition, there is a rising pattern of stress started with *and* so that the voice becomes stronger with each syllable until *in*, which drops heavily after the build-up of *broun breed*.

As noted earlier, reversals can also take place elsewhere in a line. A common place for a reversal is the third foot. Grammatical distinctions clarify the relative prominence of the syllables in question in the following line:

In pacience ladde a ful symple lyf, (VII 2826)

The unaccented final *e*'s add some complications to the scansion of this line, but starting from the rhyme word and going backward, we can construct a reading of the meter. The last syllable of *simple* is still pronounced in Modern English, and we can assume that it was pronounced also in Middle English. In this case, it receives, however, less prominence than the rhyme word:

```
                    x  /
```
In pacience ladde a ful symple lyf,

Working backwards some more, we can subordinate the stress of the qualifier *ful* to the stressed first syllable of *symple*. Starting at the beginning, we can see the preposition *in* as subordinate in stress-assignment to the first syllable of *pacience*, even though in this instance we will argue that *pacience* is pronounced here in the French manner with a tertiary stress on the first syllable. In accordance with this assumption, *pacience* will have to be seen as a word of at least three syllables. In this case, *ci* will be subordinated to *ence*, and for reasons discussed below, the final *e* will not be pronounced:

```
x  / |x/  |     |x  / | x /
```
In pacience ladde a ful symple lyf,

The remaining syllables point to a reversed foot with a silent final *e* on *ladde*:

> x /lx/   l/   xl x / l x /
> In pacience ladde a ful symple lyf,

The alternatives to this scansion seem somewhat less satisfactory. A two-syllabled *pacience* or a three-syllabled one with a pronounced silent *e* gets us into trouble. In the first instance, we end up with a two-syllable *ladde*, which is acceptable in and of itself, but we also end up with *a* as a stressed syllable:

> x /l x   / l x/lx / l x /
> In pacience ladde a ful symple lyf,

Such a reading is possible, but not probable. The third foot is distressingly light. In the case of the three-syllabled *pacience* with a sounded final *e*, we end up with an unnecessary anapest:

> x /l x/l x /   lx x / l x /
> In pacience ladde a ful symple lyf,

While anapests are acceptable substitutions in Chaucer's verse, they are generally motivated by phonological conditions not present in this line.

It is also possible for there to be reversals in the other feet of the line, although they are very rare. The reversal in the following line is debatable:

> To han housbondes hardy, wise, and free, (VII 2914)

The first, fourth, and fifth feet are very easy to understand (if we do not sound the final *e* of *wise* in light of its juxtaposition with a following vowel). Counting the final *-es* of *housbondes*, we can also account for the third foot:

> x / l   l x /l x / l x   /
> To han housbondes hardy, wise, and free,

We are left, however, with the first two syllables of *housbondes*. It is normally assumed that ancient compounds such as this receive stress on the first element. As we have seen, however, we can often assume that Chaucer varied such stress patterns at line ends to accommodate rhyme promotion. However, I think that we must distinguish rhyme promotion from mere intralineal metrical promotion. In addition, in this case, we have some alliteration that underscores the metrical burden of the stressed syllables, and the reversed foot receives emphasis from this alliteration. The only solution possible here is to scan the foot as a trochee:

x / | /　x | x / | x　/　|x　/
To han housbondes hardy, wise, and free,

Reversals may also occur in the fourth foot, but their occurrence is very rare. Indeed, when one finds what he thinks may be a reversed fourth foot, he often discovers that the line in question can be scanned in a couple of ways. The following example, however, is reasonably clear in its presentation of the phenomenon:

Of studie took he moost cure and moost heede.　(I 303)

To end up with a reversed fourth foot, we make the following judgments. We allow the first syllable of *heede* to have a metrical stress as a noun and as a rhyme word. The final *e* is sounded as a line-final *e* in a feminine rhyme. The second *moost,* an adjective, is subordinated then to the first syllable of *heede,* the headword of the noun phrase. Starting at the head of the line, we read the first syllable of *studie* as more metrically prominent than the preceding preposition, *of.* The second syllable of *studie* (the *e* seems not to be sounded here) is subordinate to the preterite verb *took.* In the case of the third foot, the qualifier *moost* has dominance over *he,* a pronoun out of normal word order. So far the scansion looks like this:

x　/| x /　|x　/　|　　| x　/　|x
Of studie took he moost cure and moost heede.

With the problem foot isolated like this, the reversal is easy to see. The monosyllabic noun *cure* has more metrical burden than the conjunction *and.* Of course, someone could argue that the conjunction could have prominence for some rhetorical purpose, but since the two characterizations of the Clerk's studiousness are more or less synonymous, the *and* seems to have little rhetorical force. A creative scanner, however, could offer another solution for the line. He could introduce an anapest through demotion of the first *moost* and then force the sounding of the *e* on *cure*:

x　/| x /　| x x　　/|x /　| x　/ | x
Of studie took he moost cure and moost heede.

This scansion is not bad, but there are some Chaucerians who frown heavily on the idea of anapests in Chaucer. But some also frown at the notion of a reversed fourth foot. I find the reversal satisfying as a rhetorically apt solution. The reversal serves to mark the fastidiousness of the Clerk's study habits.

As we have noted, the anapest is not always accepted as a viable substitution in

Chaucer, but I think that the anapest occurs in Chaucer's verse. Indeed, it is often a part of the charm of his verse. Many traditional Chaucerians (cf. French, Licklider, Skeat, and Ten Brink) prefer to devise methods of slurring and elision to solve these "problems," but these solutions are worse than the "problems." As intellectual exercises for understanding the conditions under which anapestic tendencies in a line occur, the metrical conceptions of elision and slurring are useful, but they demand a rigor of composition that denies a certain amount of freedom to a poet. Although we have argued that meter is an abstract pattern useful for composition, we cannot forget that rhythm, as a product of performance, is an important aspect of poetic form. Whether we like the idea or not, there are isochronous tendencies in English verse. The isochronism is not as rigid as musical rhythm, but there is a tendency for timing patterns to develop. With this more or less isochronous tendency, the verse can easily handle an occasional foot of three syllables. To slur these syllables seems to me to be an aberration of a very useful device and a denial of a very strong tradition in English versification.

Let's look at a variety of possible anapestic feet and see under what conditions anapests are likely to occur. The most common environment is that of a combination of two vowels, one having a close relative in a semiconsonant. The vowel represented by *y* often occurs in anapestic feet:

```
x    /  |  x/  | x  /| x x   /  | x  /
In which she eet ful many a sklendre meel.  (VII 2833)
```

The traditional solution to the anapest in a line like this is to read the *y* as the phoneme /j/, the first phoneme in a word like *yet*. The semiconsonant is then tied to the following vowel to make one syllable. Although this solution is by and large reasonable, it requests the reader to go through considerable trouble to anticipate a phonological change conditioned by the metrical pattern—although I will be the first to admit that such a conditioned change is not unusual in metrics. According to my own sense of aesthetics, I prefer to read the foot as anapestic: a pleasant change from a highly iambic pattern. In recent years, however, a suggestion has been made that the anapest is actually very prevalent in Chaucer's meter (Conner). This suggestion has been made as one method of incorporating all of Chaucer's final *e*'s. Indeed, the writer suggests that all final consonants in Chaucer's English ended in reduced vowels. Although the writer discounts many of these final reduced vowels when they precede other vowels, the resulting number of anapests seems a little too large.

The traditional view of anapests as slurs and elisions gains support in light of other phonological situations. While the conditions under which *y* assumes the semivowel form are fairly clear, the conditions under which *w* operates are a little more complicated. In the case of *w*, which is normally a semiconsonant, a preceding or following vowel has to be reduced or deleted in order for the /w/ to be juxtaposed to the vowel of the first syllable of the following word. In this example, a final *e*, which must have been otherwise pronounced, must be reduced in order to accommodate the traditional slur—I have scanned the line with an anapest, however:

    x   / l x x   /   lx / l x /   l x / lx
    This wydwe, of which I telle yow my tale, (VII 2824)

In view of the syntactic break across the slur, the reduction of the two syllables to one seems bizarre to me, and the example tests the limits of such slurring. The next example shows how a vowel preceding the *w* would be reduced in order to save the iambic foot:

    x / l x   / l x / lx /l x   x   /
    His colour was bitwixe yelow and reed, (VII 2902)

Following my own preference, I have scanned the line with an anapest. The logic of the traditional slur is partly based on the alternate spelling of the word *yelow* as *yelwe*. Someone could object to this anapest on another ground. It may be possible to demand a reversed fourth foot:

    x / l x   / l x / l / x lx   /
    His colour was bitwixe yelow and reed,

In such a scansion, however, I think we have to add a pause between *twix* and *ye*. A rhythmical principle we will develop in chapter seven will go into detail about this pause, but in short, we can say that when two metrical stresses are juxtaposed, English has a tendency to insert a pause between the two stresses. In this case, we are back with what we started: instead of an unaccented *e*, we have a pause that for better or worse still throws the equivalent of two unaccented syllables together in what surely takes on the feel of an anapest.

Other cases of anapests are also reduced to slurs or elisions by traditionalists when a liquid or an *h* is present. The most famous line with an anapest or an elision comes early in *The General Prologue*:

    x / lx / lx   / lx /l x x   / lx
    Of Engelond to Caunterbury they wende, (I 16)

The traditionalist would elide the *u* preceding the *r* with the result that a syllable somewhat in the form of /bri/ would get the fourth accent. It is notable—though not conclusive—that within the next dozen lines the word *Caunterbury* occurs twice, both times with four syllables and a stress on the *u*.

The case of the *h* depends on the notion that the *h* was often not pronounced in Middle English, and if spelling is any indication, such may have been the case. In the cases in question, a preceding vowel is slurred across the unpronounced *h* with the following vowel:

x   /l x   / lx x/ lx /lx /
Whan humours been to habundant in a wight. (VII 2925)

Once again, I have scanned the line with an anapest, preferring the anapest to the combination of the two syllables into one. In the poetry of the seventeenth century, this sort of slurring is signaled by spelling, and perhaps this practice reinforces the traditional conception. These kinds of judgments are determined by taste; I have a preference for the anapest, despite its ugly name.

Another area of dispute in Chaucer is the headless line (Freudenberger and Hammond). A headless line lacks the unaccented syllable in the first foot of the line. This lack of the unaccented syllable is best understood in rhythmic terms as the lack of anacrusis (the off-beat before the first beat of the measure). In music, the bar signals that the following note is accented, unless the composer chooses to syncopate or shift the accent. Thus, the accented note marks the beginning of the measure. In a rhythmical understanding of verse, the first accent in essence starts the first measure of the verse. In this case, the foot is a non-essential element, so the first element of the foot is inconsequential. It can be there or not, according to the poet's discretion. In a great number of cases, the first element of the iamb is present in Chaucer's verse; however, despite the iambic nature of the verse, as we have remarked before, rhythm plays an important part in Chaucer's verse. Thus, the verse will often display the characteristics of a rhythmic artifact. One such characteristic is the disappearance of the anacrusis or first element of the iamb.

If there is any aspect of Chaucer's verse that is slippery, it is the headless line. The fact of the matter is that a scanner can usually find another solution for the line through some kind of machination. We have thus arrived at what appears to be another article of faith. Here is an example of a headless line:

(x)/ l x /lx   / l x /lx /
Al bismotered with his habergeon, (I 76)

The only other scansions I can see for the line disturb my sense of English stress assignment:

/   xl x/lx   / l x /lx   /
/   xl /xlx   / l x /lx   /
x /l x/lx   / l x /lx   /
Al bismotered with his habergeon,

The first scansion asks us to accent a highly unlikely syllable. The second asks for two reversals in a row. The third suffers the same problem as the first. The easiest solution is to accept the headless line as a fact of Chaucer's verse.

Some people may have difficulty accepting the existence of something like the headless line because in essence the conception requires us to believe in something that is not there. This problem is even more acute when the metrical caesura is introduced as an aspect of Chaucer's verse. The metrical caesura is much like a rest in music and is not to be confused with the classical caesura, a syntactic break in a line with nevertheless the proper number of syllables. Although a metrical caesura may co-occur with a classical caesura, they must be kept separate in our minds. Late nineteenth- and early twentieth-century prosodists delighted in accounting for all of the classical caesurae in Chaucer (cf. Schipper), and these prosodists referred to these caesurae as "heroic" caesurae because of their existence in the heroic verses of France. The heroic caesura is merely a break in the line:

> x / l x / l x ^ /   l x / l x / l x
> To ferne halwes, kowthe in sondry londes; (I 14)

I have marked the heroic caesura with a caret. This caesura occurs at a syntactic break, and the editor of our text has marked the break with a comma. In Chaucer's fifteenth-century manuscripts, a virgule (/) often marks the heroic caesura, and the mark has come under much scrutiny in recent years. Indeed, some have believed that the mark is integral to an understanding of Chaucer's meter (cf. Southworth). But to the more conservative, the use of the virgule by the scribes seems inconsistent and often arbitrary. However, modern scholars have used the virgule to obscure the nature of Chaucer's verse, making it look like alliterative meter—without the alliteration. But lacking a Chaucerian holograph, we will have to regard the placement of the virgules as interesting but unreliable.

The kind of caesura that we are interested in here is a purely metrical phenomenon. It is in essence a musical rest that fills a position in a line. The notion of a metrical caesura rests on the assumption that isochronism develops in a reading of Chaucer's verse. The metrical caesura is a hard thing to find, however, and other solutions can be suggested for the lines in question. The following line can be scanned with a metrical caesura:

> x   /   l x   / l(x) /   l / x l x /
> As seyde hymself, moore than a curat, (I 219)

This is not the only way to scan the line, however. Someone with a preference for anapests could let them gallop forth to give us a sense of the sweetness of the voice of the indirectly quoted Friar:

x /   Ix x   /   I(x)/   Ix /   Ix x/
As seyde hymself, moore than a curat,

As I offer these scansions with the metrical caesura, I do ask the indulgence of the reader. I beg him to read the line with the pause to see how it sounds. If the pause still seems distasteful, try the following "straight" scansions, one with a reversed fourth foot and the other with an anapest:

x   / Ix / Ix   /   I / xI x/
As seyde hymself, moore than a curat,

x   / Ix / Ix   / Ix / Ix x /
As seyde hymself, moore than a curat,

I prefer the scansion with the metrical caesura because it avoids placing the first syllable of *hymself* in a stressed position. Although our notion of the foot as explained in earlier chapters handles this situation well, aspects of performance here seem to outweigh the strict compositional rules we have lauded elsewhere. Although Chaucer uses the kinds of substitutions in his iambic verse that later English poets use, he is somewhat conservative in his use of them. He seems to avoid the roughness of the fifteenth-century poets who rely heavily on the metrical caesura to fill out their "broken-backed" lines. He is not as tricky as Shakespeare with his development of character through metrical sleight of hand. Nor is he as difficult as Donne, who seems to have reveled in crabbed rhythms. The eighteenth century would have been a little stiff for Chaucer, but he might have found metrical comrades in nineteenth-century poets. Chaucer's voice is unique, however, and probably comes closer to capturing a colloquial sound in formal meter than any other poet of English. His metrical substitutions are important aids in this attempt to be colloquial, and a sensitive scanner of Chaucer's verse should acknowledge them when they appear. To do anything else is to read Chaucer with the dullest of ears.

Exercise 5.1

Directions: Scan the following lines and take special note about the substitutions that are possible and probable in them. See if you can justify the substitutions on rhetorical grounds.

1. Curteys she was, discreet, and debonaire, (VII 2871)
2. Beestes and briddes koude speke and synge. (VII 2881)
3. Seyde he nat thus, 'Ne do no fors of dremes'? (VII 2941)

4. Seynd bacoun, and somtyme an ey or tweye, (VII 2845)
5. "Avoy!" quod she, "fy on yow, hertelees! (VII 2908)
6. Nothyng, God woot, but vanitee in sweven is. (VII 2922)
7. Ful weel she soong the service dyvyne, (I 122)
8. A Monk ther was, a fair for the maistrie, (I 165)
9. That rounded as a belle out of the presse. (I 263)
10. But sikerly she hadde a fair forheed; (I 154)
11. His voys was murier than the murie orgon (VII 2851)
12. Sevene hennes for to doon al his plesaunce, (VII 2866)
13. Upon my body, and wolde han had me deed. (VII 2901)
14. Causeth ful many a man in sleep to crie (VII 2934)
15. At that tyme, for hym liste ride so, (I 102)
16. For to deelen with no swich poraille, (I 247)
17. Whan that Aprill with his shoures soote (I 1)
18. He hadde of gold ywroght a ful curious pyn; (I 196)
19. This prison caused me nat for to crye, (I 1095)
20. Is likned til a fissh that is waterlees— (I 180)

Exercise 5.1

Can the following line be read with a metrical caesura? What must be done to read the line with a metrical caesura? What substitutions can be justified? What arguments can be made for different scansions of the line?

A millere was ther dwellynge many a day. (I 3925)

References and Suggested Reading

Conner, Jack. *English Prosody from Chaucer to Wyatt.* Janua Linguarum, Series Practica, 193. The Hague: Mouton, 1974.

French, Robert D. "Versification." In *A Chaucer Handbook.* 2nd ed. New York: Appleton-Century-Crofts, 1947. 362-67.

Freudenberger, Markus. *Über das Fehlen des Auftakts in Chaucers heroischem Verse.* 1889; rpt. Amsterdam: Editions Rodopi, 1970.

Hammond, Eleanor Prescott. "Linguistics and Versification." In *Chaucer: A Bibliographical Manual.* New York: Peter Smith, 1933. 464-509.

Licklider, Albert H. *Chapters on the Metric of the Chaucerian Tradition.* Baltimore: J. H. Furst, 1910.

Schipper, Jakob. *A History of English Versification.* 1910; rpt. New York: AMS Press, 1971.

Skeat, Walter W. "An Essay on the Language and Versification of Chaucer." Part the Third, vii-xv. *The Poetical Works of Geoffrey Chaucer.* Ed. Richard Morris. Rev. ed. London: Bell and Daldy, 1872. I, 172-96.

Southworth, James G. *The Prosody of Chaucer and His Followers: Supplementary Chapters to* Verses of Cadence. 1962; rpt. Westport, Conn.: Greenwood Press, 1978.

——. *Verses of Cadence: An Introduction to the Prosody of Chaucer and His Followers.* Oxford: Basil Blackwell, 1954.

Ten Brink, Bernhard. *The Language and Metre of Chaucer.* 2nd ed. Rev. by Friedrich Kluge. Trans. by M. Bentinck Smith. 1901; rpt. New York: Haskell House, 1968.

Six: Chaucer's Four-Stress Meter

Iambic pentameter is the meter of Chaucer's mature poetic days. According to our best guesses about chronology, however, the four-stress meter was Chaucer's choice for longer works in his earlier days. In ideal form, the meter is essentially iambic tetrameter—lines of eight syllables in a pattern of unstress-stress. Granting Chaucer the line-final unaccented *e*, the line is generally nine syllables long. Chaucer's model for the four-stress was probably the French octosyllabic line, popular in French for romances and the greatly influential work *Le Roman de la Rose*. Disputes persist among scholars about whether or not the medieval French line had a pattern of unstress-stress, but whatever the outcome of the dispute, Middle English writers who attempted to copy the French romancers adopted a more or less eight-syllabled line with four stresses.

The line as we have it in Chaucer is often awkward, but Chaucer succeeds in creating poetic beauty with the line despite its limitations (Clemen, Malone, Shannon, and Thompson). In English at any rate, the line has a tendency to become isochronous. The rhythm of four beats is very catchy, and thus the meter has a tendency to run roughshod over the words. A related tendency of the meter is the promotion of stresses and the demotion of unstresses to the point that the unstressed positions are filled with no syllables or with two (and perhaps three) syllables. Because of this heavy demotion and promotion, scansion of the four-stress meter is often very difficult. A considerable amount of fiddling has to go on in some cases to get the lines to scan, and then optional scansions may seem equally applicable. Sometimes lines could reasonably have only three stresses; at other times, the lines could reasonably have five. If we discount scribally corrupt lines, however, the application of substitutions can resolve the difficult lines.

It is probably silly to think of the ideal form of Chaucer's four-stress line as iambic tetrameter because the eight-syllable version is very rare. The hypermetric version with a line-final unaccented *e* is the preponderant form. However, it is useful for pedagogical purposes to look closely at a "neutral" line. I offer the following example:

And, also domb as any stoon, (HF 656)

We proceed with the scansion of the four-stress line in the same manner in which we scanned the five-stress line. The rhyme syllable, *stoon*, receives stress for the convention of rhyme and for its prominence as a noun over the unstressed syllable of *any*. The correlative conjunction *as* falls in with the first syllable of *any* as an iambic foot. *domb* takes prominence as an adjective over the second syllable of *also*. Assuming that the main stress of *also* is applied to the first syllable, *al-* takes prominence over *And*. The results of these stress assignments follow:

    x   /ǀ x /   ǀx /ǀx /
    And, also domb as any stoon,

Alternate scansions would hardly be satisfactory in this case.

The unaccented *e* also figures in the scansion of the four-stress line. In many cases, it is difficult to argue against the pronunciation of the *e*, for it is part of a living inflection. These two lines offer examples of sounded *e*'s as part of verbal inflections:

    As burned gold hyt shoon to see;

    And soth to tellen, also she (HF 1387-88)

In the first line, the stresses line up fairly easily. The infinitive *see* takes prominence over the infinitive marker *to*. The preterite *shoon* takes prominence over the pronoun *hyt*. *burn*, part of an adjectival past participial, has prominence over *As*. These assignments leave us with the line in this shape:

    x   / ǀ   ǀx /   ǀx /
    As burned gold hyt shoon to see;

In the remaining foot, *gold* obviously deserves a stress, and we have to assume that the *-ed* is pronounced. If it is not, we would have to assume that what we have here is a metrical caesura. But a metrical caesura should only be assumed when no other solution is available, and considering that the *-ed* is apparently pronounced in even later poetry, we do no violence to taste or to historical phonology to scan the syllable as the unstressed member of the second foot.

The second line can be resolved in a similar way. The rhyme syllable *she* takes prominence over the second syllable of *also*. The noun *soth* takes prominence over the conjunction *And*. *tell-* commands prominence over the infinitive marker *to*. The line takes this form at this point:

```
x    /  |x /|    |x  /
```
And soth to tellen, also she

It would belabor the issue to avoid seeing that the line would limp unnecessarily without sounding the infinitive ending.

The use of unaccented *e*'s in Chaucer's four-stress verse parallels its use in his five-stress verse. As in the cases above, the *e*'s can be part of viable inflectional systems, but the *e*'s can also be parts of vestigial systems of inflection or, as we saw before, the results of linguistic analogy or confusion. Historical perspectives on the source of the *e* are not as important as the mere fact of the existence of the *e* as a phonological variation available to Chaucer. Without the *e*, the following line would be a metrical disaster:

So moche beaute, trewely, (BD 1197)

If we assume that we have four stresses in the line, two stresses can be established on grammatical grounds (*beaut-* and *trew-*); one we grant on metrical grounds (the rhyme syllable -*ly*); and one we acknowledge with some trepidation (*moch-*). But the line still has problems unless we scan the unaccented *e*'s. One has immediate historical justification: the final *e* of *beaute*. The word is a borrowing from French, and in French the final *e* is pronounced (and accented) as part of a nominal suffix. In addition, the word as it survives in Modern English, *beauty*, has a pronounced second syllable. Grammatical arguments could be erected in the case of *moche*, but I think the simplest solution to apply here and in the case of the *e* in *trewely* is one of stress-timing. The variant pronunciations were available to Chaucer, and he used them in these instances. With the application of these considerations, we have a regular line of iambic tetrameter:

```
x  /| x /  |x  /| x/
```
So moche beaute, trewely,

The line may seem bizarre to the twentieth-century ear, but such lines are so common that they must have seemed perfectly acceptable to Chaucer.

Allowance must also be made for Chaucer's line-final unaccented *e*. As in the iambic pentameter, a great number of four-stress lines end with hypermetric syllables. The name *hypermetric* is thus probably a misnomer; perhaps *hypometric* should be adopted for the lines that lack the final unstressed syllable. The feminine rhyme is certainly allowable in pairs like the following:

```
  x  /  lx  /   l   x  / lx   / l x
```
Why this a drem, why that a sweven,

```
  x     /    l x/  l x  /  l x    / lx
```
And noght to every man lyche even; (HF 9-10)

In this example, we clearly have a final unstressed syllable at the end of each line. Although words like *even* are often reduced in English poetry to one-syllable contractions like *e'en*, I do not believe that Chaucer is asking us to do so here. Such a reduction might also be convenient in the case of an anapest, but even there I believe that the word is multisyllabic. A perceptive reader might note that a contraction has been used in the case of *every*, but such a contraction is certainly justified by the usual pronunciation of the Modern English form of the word. If someone prefers to scan the line in question with an anapest, I will not protest. The practice of easily recognizable feminine rhymes also appears in lines from which Lord Byron must have learned something:

```
  x   /l x /  l x    /l x  / l x
```
Of tymes of hem, ne the causes,

```
  x     / l x   / lx  /  l x  /    lx
```
Or why this more then that cause is— (HF 19-20)

Here *ryme riche* (identical rhyming words usually of different grammatical functions) is complicated by the use of a reduced form of the copula to rhyme with the plural suffix.

More likely than not, the usual form of the hypermetric line has one or both final syllables pronounced without firm historical information, but historical clues and aesthetics provide the justification for sounding the final *e*'s in the following:

```
  x /  lx  /  l x /  lx  /l x
```
That yt forwot that ys to come,

```
  x    /  l x  /l x  /  lx   /l x
```
And that hyt warneth alle and some (HF 45-46)

The reduced infinitive suffix, which may not be pronounced elsewhere, is here sounded like the final syllable of the indefinite pronoun. As we argued for the iambic pentameter line, the reader is ultimately the judge of whether or not to scan the hypermetric syllable. The reader knows where I stand.

The looseness of Chaucer's four-stress line admits many substitutions. In terms of trochaic inversions, for example, the four-stress line seems to admit substitutions at just about any place in the line. We find them in the first foot a considerable number of times. Many of these instances can be disputed for one reason or another, but rhetorical redundancy and alliteration argue for the promotion of the adverb over the preposition in the following line:

     /   x I x /I x   / I x / I x
     Doun fro the heven gan descende, (HF 164)

Grammatical importance certainly makes the verb more prominent than the preposition in the next example:

     /   x I x   / I x / Ix   /
     Made of hym shortly at oo word (HF 257)

Syntactic parallelism and other rhetorical considerations prompt the inversion in this instance:

     / x I x   /   I x / I x   / I x
     Al hir compleynt ne al hir moone, (HF 362)

We may have a rhetorical choice in this line, allowing us to invert or not to invert:

     /   x Ix /I x   / Ix /
     Loo, how a woman doth amys (HF 269)

Following the same considerations, we can find inversions in other positions in the line. An inversion in the second foot appears, for example, in this uncharacteristically heavy line:

     x   / I/ x Ix   / I x   /
     Lyght thing upward, and dounward charge. (HF 746)

Perhaps here we get an onomatopoeic effect of the labor of flight in the heavy adjective-noun foot followed by the inversion. The third foot also sports inversions, and despite the position of the third foot near the end of the line, it becomes very commonplace to find an inversion. In the following example, we have inverted third feet in two contiguous lines. The second line is obviously related to the last example we offered:

```
  x   /  | x   /   | /   x | x  / | x
```
And with this word, soth for to seyne,

```
  x  /  |x  /   |/   x  |x / | x
```
He gan alway upper to sore, (HF 960-61)

In the first line, grammatical and rhetorical considerations justify the inversion—and the alliteration is nice. In the second, the root of the word *upper* is promoted over the suffix (*alway* receives stress on the second syllable here as it often seems to receive; if we invert this foot, the labor of flight is certainly well portrayed in metrical complexity). The question of reversed fourth feet is excluded from this discussion because of the prejudice of the author. However, someone who does not believe that rhyming syllables have to have a strong stress can certainly invert to his heart's content in the fourth foot. Here I prefer the strength of the meter to the strength of word accent.

Anapests are also very frequent in occurrence in Chaucer's four-stress verse. This frequent occurrence of the anapest is an indication that the metrical conception of the four-stress line is different from that of the five-stress line. The four-stress line, as noted above, has isochronous tendencies, and although the direction of causation is unclear and probably irrelevant, the anapests result from and reinforce the isochronous tendency. The anapests may occur in any foot in the line, but anapests in the first foot are considerably rarer than those in other feet. The problem with the first foot is that since there is nothing with which to compare the first element of the foot until another syllable or so has gone by, it is difficult to tell right off what the first foot is. Sometimes, the anapest in the first foot is arrived at by default: we assume that all the lines are in four-stress meter; a possible fifth stress in the line has to be demoted. Here is a good example of the problem:

Whether hyt were clere or hors of soun. (BD 347)

Starting from the end, we clarify the scansion of the easy portions of the line. The noun *soun* takes prominence over the preposition *of*; the adjective *hors* does the same over the conjunction *or*. Now things get tricky. On grammatical grounds, we can argue that the first syllable (of two possible syllables) of the adjective *clere* will probably be assigned a metrical stress. With this assumption, we can extend our argument and say that one of the two possible syllables of *were* will be the unstressed member of the foot that contains *clere*. We conclude that the final *e* of *clere* is not sounded in this instance: one, it is not necessary for the scansion; two, scanning it would require us to grant a hiatus between the *e* and initial vowel of *or*. Further, seeing that we still have a plethora of syllables to account for, we can dispose of the final *e* of *were*. So far, we have the following scansion:

```
 | x    /  |x  /  |x  /
```
Whether hyt were clere or hors of soun.

With three possible syllables left, we have three options. One, we can reduce *Whether* to a one-syllable word, an option that has phonological justification in Middle English. However, when it is clear that the word is monosyllabic, it is spelled that way ("And *wher* my lord, my love, be deed?" BD 91). Two, we could read the first foot as a trochaic inversion and the second foot as an anapest. This scansion, however, leaves us with an unfortunate string of three unstressed syllables, a sort of string, however, that may appear elsewhere in Chaucer's four-stress lines. Three, we can say that the foot is anapestic. This judgment requires us to smooth over the stress contrast of the dissyllabic word, but since the word has a variant monosyllabic form, it is easy to demote the initial syllable for the sake of the meter. I vote for the third solution and complete the scansion in this manner:

```
  x  x   /  | x    /   |x  /   |x  /
```
Whether hyt were clere or hors of soun.

This is clearly an ambiguous example, but characteristic in the problems it presents in lines with initial anapests. Perhaps a simpler example is in order:

Ne in ayr ne in erthe noon element, (BD 694)

Once again, it is easier to start at the end of the line. The last two feet are not a problem: the rhyme syllable *-ment* has prominence over the second syllable of *element*, and the initial syllable of the word has prominence as the stressed syllable of a noun over a preceding quantifier. Such assignments leave us with two feet to clarify. Obvious choices for the stresses are the nouns *ayr* and *erthe*. The final *e* on *erthe* is not necessary for the scansion, so we can assume that it is not sounded. We are left then with two parallel syntactic structures that for the sake of the meter must be a pair of anapests:

```
  x  x  /   |x  x  /    |x    /| x  /
```
Ne in ayr ne in erthe noon element,

There are two arguments against these anapests. One, elsewhere a stress-contrast could be established for a pair of words like *ne in*. However, in this case, we smooth over the contrast to sustain the four-stress meter. Two, elision or slurring could be invoked to reduce the two words to one syllable much in the manner of the usual Chaucerian *ne + is = nis*. However, this combination is not presented in the spelling, and it is not a common contraction. However, the phonological tendency of Middle English to make such contractions gives us permission as it were to accept the anapest as an unobtrusive substitution here. It is also interesting to note that in the last example under question, we have a line with two anapests, a relatively common thing in Chaucer's four-stress meter.

The last example shows an anapest in the second foot, but anapests can also be found in the second foot and in other feet as the sole anapests of a line. Here is a clear example of an anapest in the second foot:

         x   / lx   x /l x / l x   /
         Such sorowe this lady to her tok (BD 95)

It would be difficult to provide any kind of elision or slurring here. Anapests also appear in the third foot:

         x   /l x   / l x x /l x   /
         And reson gladly she understood; (BD 1011)

Once again, it would be difficult to suggest a different scansion. The anapestic substitution also appears in the last foot of the line. Many of the examples available are parts of somewhat arhythmic lines, but this example reads well:

         x / l x   / l x / l x x /l x
         That al hir wyt was set, by the rode, (BD 992)

The frequency of the anapest in the four-stress line thus gives the meter great rhythmic flexibility.

This flexibility extends to great numbers of headless lines. In fact, the great number of headless lines makes the scansion of the four-stress lines difficult at times. When a line starts off on an odd member of a foot, it takes a while for the unwitting scanner to recover the rhythm of the line. In the matter of headless lines more than in any other matter, authorial intention would be nice to know. Although we can establish headlessness after some analysis, often it would be nice to know what to expect as we read the verse—not as a syllable-by-syllable exercise in historical phonology—but as a poem delivered with some dramatic interpretation. Plodding in our historical-phonological way, however, we can decide a lot to help a second reading make rhythmic sense. Here is an example that illustrates what can happen to an unwitting reader:

         "But wherfore that I telle thee

         Whan I first my lady say? (BD 1088-89)

A reader who innocently reads the first line as an example of regular iambic tetrameter might be tempted to continue the pattern in the next line, where he would come to a screeching halt in the second foot:

    x   / | x   / | x / | x /
    "But wherfore that I telle thee

    x / | x   ? / | x /
    Whan I first my lady say?

With such a start in the line, the reader has placed himself in an inextricable mess unless he backs up and reconsiders what has happened. Once again, working backwards gives some perspective. The last foot scans satisfactorily, and if we back up two syllables and place *my* with *la-*, we can establish another foot. Backing up again, we place *I* next to *first*, and the adverb gains prominence over the pronoun if for no other reason than that it establishes the importance of the initial meeting of the two lovers. With these three feet established, we have recourse to a foot lacking an unstressed syllable—a headless line:

    (x)   / | x / | x / | x /
       Whan I first my lady say?

Objections may be raised to this scansion. One, we may actually have a line of three feet with an initial anapest:

    x x / | x / | x /
    Whan I first my lady say?

However, we would have to admit here that Chaucer had lapsed into ballad meter. Such a lapse is possible since four-stress couplets with their isochronism can easily fall into couplets of four and three, but I think we may prefer to say that Chaucer has kept to the steady meter that he uses clearly just about everywhere in the poem. Two, a dramatic reading could offer the first two words as an iamb and then insert a metrical caesura between *I* and *first*:

    x / |(x) / | x / | x /
    Whan I   first my lady say?

This is a satisfying reading, but it asks us to read the line with a metrical contraption that we may not need. The simplest solution is to scan the line as headless, and we have the satisfaction of knowing that the contraption that we are using is very common in Chaucer's four-stress poetry.

However, there are times when the metrical caesura is a welcome addition to our repertoire of scanning devices. If commonness is a criterion worthy of consideration, I believe that we can say that the metrical caesura—in the traditional foot scansion we have offered—is more frequently observed in Chaucer's four-stress meter than in his five-stress meter. The reason for this is obvious: the isochronism of the four-stress meter. Wherever we find a metrical caesura, someone could offer complaints against it, but the following example presents a metrical caesura in a logical syntactic position:

> "What los ys that?" quod I thoo; (BD 1139)

The scansion here can begin from either direction and, in fact, runs into a problem from whichever direction it starts. Starting from the back, we can give prominence to the rhyme word *thoo* and demote the pronoun *I* to give us a fourth foot. If we continue backwards, however, the next foot may be fine, but we soon end up with a mess containing either a reversed foot following a headless foot or a noun heavily demoted in favor of a heavily promoted copula after the headless foot. Some of this mess can be avoided by starting at the beginning of the line after establishing the last foot. Then we get three very regular feet. The results so far look like this:

> x / |x   / | |x   /
> "What los ys that?" quod I thoo;

The way out of the conundrum then presented by the lack of a syllable in the middle of the line is to provide a metrical caesura, justified on rhythmic and syntactic grounds. A pause is logical between a direct quotation and the speaker tag:

> x / |x   / | (x) / |x /
> "What los ys that?" quod I thoo;

The solution is simply aesthetically pleasing. What more could we ask of a scansion? There are other metrical caesurae whose existence we could argue, and I believe that our arguments are valid when they have syntactic and aesthetic justifications.

Before leaving this discussion of the four-stress line, we must say something about the combination of metrical effects. A headless line often has an anapest somewhere else in the line:

> (x) /| x /|x   x / |x /
> By the maner me thoghte so— (BD 453)

A more tin-eared reader may prefer to scan the line as regular. Although I grant that a determiner can have prominence over the initial syllable of a dissyllabic noun (or trisyllabic noun with a final *e*) at the end of the line where the second syllable of the noun is accented for rhyme (BD 605), I think that in general such a scansion should be avoided elsewhere in the line. There are a couple of reasons, however, that we can give for the frequency of the headless line with an anapest. One, Chaucer may have very well been counting syllables sometimes without worrying too much about stress position. Two, there may be underlying metrical rules for compensation in rhythmical verse, a subject for the next chapter. However, we may quickly note other combinations of substitutions with little comment. We can spot numbers of lines with both trochees and anapests:

>   / x l x / l x x /   lx /   lx
> Whethir so men wil portreye or peynte, (BD 783)

A headless line can also have a trochee:

> (x) / l x / l /   xl x / lx
> That was lyk noon of the route; (BD 819)

Finally, it is possible to have two trochees in a line:

>   / x l x   /l / x lx   /l x
> Ever to be stedfast and trewe, (BD 1227)

Chaucer's four-stress meter, as we can see, is very supple and flexible. Chaucer abandoned it in his later works, but he employed it with a master's skill. When he developed his five-stress narrative line, he already possessed a metrical vehicle for longer poems that served his purposes well. Perhaps, however, Chaucer abandoned the four-stress line because of its tendency to become too musical. The five-stress line frustrates the tendency to make groups of twos, threes, and fours into musically rhythmical units. The five-stress line forces rhythmic breaks into alternating groups of twos and threes. When it becomes musically rhythmical, it develops patterns of four over the recurrent five-stress pattern as established by the pattern of feet.

Exercise 6.1

Directions: Scan the following regular lines.

1. For in this region, certeyn, (HF 929)

2. But wher in body or in gost (HF 981)
3. I not, ywys, but God, thou wost," (HF 982)
4. "Nay, certeynly," quod y, "ryght naught." (HF 994)
5. "And why?" "For y am now to old." (HF 995)
6. "Now up the hed, for al ys wel; (HF 1021)
7. As most conservatyf the soun. (HF 847)
8. Of labour and devocion (HF 666)
9. "O wel-away that I was born! (HF 345)
10. And how the tempest al began, (HF 435)

Exercise 6.2

Directions: Scan the following lines. Note how the unaccented *e* functions in each line.

How fals eke was he Theseus,
That, as the story telleth us,
How he betrayed Adriane—
The devel be hys soules bane!
For had he lawghed, had he loured,
He moste have ben al devoured,
Yf Adriane ne had ybe.
And for she had of hym pite,
She made hym fro the deth escape,
And he made hir a ful fals jape; (HF 405-14)

Exercise 6.3

Directions: Identify the substitutions in the following lines. Note any ambiguities in the scansion of the lines. Assemble arguments for alternate scansions whenever possible, eliminating arguments with counterarguments.

1. He moste rede many a rowe (HF 448)
2. Thoo was I war, lo, at the laste, (HF 496)
3. Pharoo, Turnus, ne Elcanor, (HF 516)
4. And be not agast so, for shame!" (HF 557)
5. To do thys, so that thou take (HF 603)
6. And faire Venus also, (HF 618)
7. Is spoken, either privy or apert, (HF 717)

8. As I have of the watir preved, (HF 814)
9. And beheld feldes and playnes, (HF 897)
10. As the Raven or eyther Bere, (HF 1004)

References and Suggested Reading

Clemen, Wolfgang. "Chaucer's Versification." In *Chaucer's Early Poetry*. Trans. C. A. M. Sym. London: Methuen, 1963. 63-66.

Malone, Kemp. "Chaucer's 'Book of the Duchess': A Metrical Study." In Arno Esch, ed. *Chaucer und seine Zeit: Symposion für Walter F. Schirmer*. Tübingen: Max Niemeyer, 1968. 71-95.

Shannon, Edgar F. "Chaucer's Use of the Octosyllabic Verse in *The Book of the Duchess* and *The House of Fame*." *JEGP* 12 (1913): 277-94.

Thompson, Elbert N. S. "The Octosyllabic Couplet." *Philological Quarterly* 18 (1939): 257-68.

Seven: Metrical Abstraction and Rhythmic Realization

As we discussed in chapter one, meter is an abstraction that the poet uses to organize differences in syllable stress. Lines of poetry rarely realize the meter in its "ideal" form; indeed, poets vary the make-up of lines both as concessions to the nature of language and as attempts at aesthetic effects. Thus, it is useful to think of meter as a compositional device: something that the poet uses to control the pattern of stresses in his verse. The meter of a poem may be very obtrusive and force the syllables of the lines into heavy demotions or promotions, or it may be very unobtrusive with an almost cantankerous resistance to regularity. Much great English poetry lies somewhere in between these two extremes. Chaucer's does.

We also discussed rhythm as recurrent events in space or time. Meter is in essence a kind of rhythm. When the meter is obtrusive and isochronous in nature, the verse will very nearly conform to the rhythm dictated by the metrical abstraction. On the other hand, the rhythm of a freer meter may not always correspond to the pattern of the metrical abstraction. When a line has light stresses or heavy unstresses, the pulse of the line may not clearly reflect the ideal pattern of the meter. This in effect is what often happens in Chaucer's verse. While the lines in Chaucer's iambic pentameter are generally justifiable examples of the meter in question, a given performance of his verse may be delivered in rhythms that do not correspond to the five-stress pulse. This phenomenon occurs because metrical stress and linguistic stress are not the same things. There are two useful ways of looking at this interesting lack of correspondence between the meter and the rhythm of Chaucer's lines. One way (which has unfortunately received more dogmatic treatment than it should have) is to view Chaucer's verse as strong-stress meter: meter determined merely by numbers of linguistic stresses. The other way is a method developed by Derek Attridge in *The Rhythm of English Poetry*. Although Attridge devotes no more than passing references to Chaucer's verse, his loosely isochronous method of scansion can be usefully employed to distinguish the basic differences between the rhythms of Chaucer's four- and five-stress meters and to account for the realization of the meter as performed rhythm.

Although some prosodists find the strong-stress readings of Chaucer's five-stress meter difficult to stomach, I think that in some sense the readings give us a better appreciation of Chaucer's verse (Robertson). To say that the readings are the only way to scan Chaucer's verse is ludicrous, for the fact of the matter is that Chaucer has a definitely recurring meter. However, it is interesting to note how the strong stresses shape the performance of the line and figure into rhythmic schemes. A scanner intent on finding four-stress lines in *The Canterbury Tales*, for example, has little trouble scanning fairly pleasant four-stress verse:

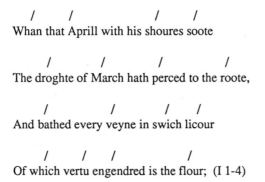

```
    /      /                /      /
Whan that Aprill with his shoures soote

        /        /         /          /
The droghte of March hath perced to the roote,

      /           /          /     /
And bathed every veyne in swich licour

      /     /   /             /
Of which vertu engendred is the flour;  (I 1-4)
```

The scansion suppresses the bumps, however slight, of the scannable prepositions *with* in line 1 and *to* in line 2, the quantifying determiner *every* in line 3, and the linking verb *is* in line 4, but strong-stress meter allows such strings of unstressed syllables between stressed ones. The reader will get the full effect of the line if he reads it in a musical rhythm, making the strong stresses the first beat of a measure. In such a performance of these lines, it is interesting to note the strings of three unstressed syllables in the lines (where the forgotten stresses are) and their position in regard to the strong stresses. Chaucer varies their position, and although he was thinking of fives, his ear varied arrangements of fours. The lines that we have here offer the unstressed strings after the second, the third, the first, and the third stresses in each line respectively. While this reading does not account for the meter of the lines, the results are satisfactory in terms of the aesthetics of performance. The results are so satisfactory that serious scholars and sixteenth-century poets have entertained the readings as genuine descriptions of Chaucer's meter.

Other scholars have observed that Chaucer's lines have caesurae, marked in the manuscripts by virgules (Southworth, Killough, and Robinson). Although the evidence for what exactly the virgule marked has not been satisfactorily determined, the notion of caesurae in the lines is interesting for the readings that it produces. I cite the same lines again to illustrate the reading, placing carets where it seems to me that the caesurae might go. Once again the reader should adopt a musically rhythmical style of delivery, this time leaving an appropriate rest in the place of the caesura:

/   /   ^   /   /
Whan that Aprill with his shoures soote

/   /   ^   /   /
The droghte of March hath perced to the roote,

/   / ^   /   /
And bathed every veyne in swich licour

/   /^   /   /
Of which vertu engendred is the flour;   (I 1-4)

While this kind of reading is interesting, I must admit that it gets tedious to me. I prefer a more syntactically (or metrically) motivated kind of caesura. The heavy-handedness of the above caesurae is not pleasing, especially since two of them break the lines at places where the string of unaccented syllables appear. Such kinds of jogging readings, however, have received serious attention by scholars.

A much more useful approach has been developed recently by Derek Attridge in the work mentioned above. His readings are primarily rhythmical, but he avoids many of the pitfalls of rhythmic prosodists. He does not use musical notation, a fruitful choice of methods. Musical notation, as C. S. Lewis quipped, makes a book lover uncomfortable, and it is cumbersome and expensive to work with. In addition, musical scansion promotes the isochronism of verse too heavily. Attridge does not insist on isochronism in what he considers the best English verse and so avoids a method of scansion that would promote isochronous readings. He chooses instead to read the lines as rhythmical—i. e., events in time—but not metronomical. The stresses of a line, for Attridge, thus are subject to isochronous tendencies but are not ruled by them.

Abandoning feet as poor descriptions of the rhythm of English verse, he adopts a looser notation that uses letters. Thinking in terms of beats and off-beats, he uses B for beats and o for offbeats. He signals complications in the options for positions in a line by using parentheses and brackets:

(o)   optional offbeat: neutral preference

<o>   optional offbeat: preference for inclusion

((o))   optional offbeat: preference for omission

[B]   unrealized beat

([B]) optional unrealized beat

The symbols and their definitions depend on an understanding of how English verse works. The symbol for the optional offbeat *(o)* provides a means, for example, of noting abstractly the feminine ending of five-stress verse, which can be described in its neutral form like this:

o B o B o B o B o B (o)

Chaucer's verse shows a preference for feminine endings, so for Chaucer we would choose the following abstract formula:

o B o B o B o B o B <o>

To accommodate Chaucer's habit of using headless lines, we would also use the symbol for optional offbeat with preference for inclusion:

<o> B o B o B o B o B <o>

   Although Attridge does not use feet in his system, the notion of inversion is still useful for him. In his system, an offbeat, according to the particular poet's practice, can be filled with more than one unstressed syllable. He has condition rules to specify preferences for this kind of practice, but when a line of five-stress meter begins with a beat, the beat will generally be followed by a double offbeat, symbolized as *o* with an inverted caret:

B ŏ B o B o B o B <o>

Inversions can occur elsewhere in a line, and when they occur, they are followed by double offbeats. However, Attridge argues that the resulting clash of stresses is avoided by an implied offbeat, symbolized by *o* with a caret on top:

o B o B o B ô B ŏ B <o>

This implied offbeat will seem clearer when we scan some lines from Chaucer, but it is important to note for now that a type of metrical caesura is important in Attridge's system. Such a condition accounts for the so-called double foot by placing the two unstressed syllables in an offbeat and an implied offbeat between the two stresses, in effect retaining the iambic pattern as an anapest and an iamb.

There are other symbols in Attridge's system that are useful here in our discussion. Attridge accommodates demotion and promotion. Demotion occurs for Attridge when a stressed syllable falls between two other stressed syllables or "after a line-boundary and before a stressed syllable" (359). Demotion is symbolized by an *o* with a dot over it. Promotion occurs when an unstressed syllable is between two other unstressed syllables or when it occurs between a line-boundary and a stressed syllable. Promotion is symbolized by a *B* with a line drawn over it. To more fully illustrate the processes of the scansion, Attridge places symbols over the line to show the relative linguistic stress of the syllables: +*s* symbolizes a stressed syllable; -*s* symbolizes an unstressed syllable. He adds to the annotation of stress to account for other differences, but they do not concern us here.

An application of the scansion to some of Chaucer's lines will help clarify the method. We will begin with iambic pentameter lines we have already scanned before so that we can more fully note the differences in the methods of scansion. The reader will remember the following lines from our discussion of neutral lines:

> x /| x / | x /|x / |x /
> Bifil that in that seson on a day,

> x / | x /|x /|x / |x /
> In Southwerk at the Tabard as I lay   (I 19-20)

In Attridge's terms, the lines would look like this:

> -s+s -s -s   -s +s -s -s -s +s
> Bifil that in that seson on a day,
> oB o B̄ o Bo B̄ o B

> -s +s   -s -s -s +s -s -s -s +s
> In Southwerk at the Tabard as I lay
> o B   o B̄ o Bo B̄ o B

This method of scansion, even in these more or less neutral lines, brings about a compromise between the metrical abstraction and the realized rhythm. Promotion occurs very frequently in Chaucer, and indeed it occurs four times in these two lines. This scansion notes this promotion clearly, and the result is that the reader gets both a sense of the meter and the linguistic structuring of the line in its prose rhythms. The separation of the two notions illustrates that the meter as a rhythmical pattern may be different to a degree from the pattern of linguistic stresses fulfilling the abstract pattern.

The implied offbeat condition that Attridge finds between contiguous stresses in the iambic pentameter tradition after Chaucer gives some justification to the scansion of the unaccented *e*. We earlier offered the following line as regular iambic pentameter if the unaccented *e*'s are included:

```
    x   / l x   /l x   /  l x   /l x   /
With scalled browes blake and piled berd.  (I 627)
```

If we wish to assume that all of the unaccented *e*'s are not pronounced, Attridge's system gives us a means of accommodating the missing offbeats as implied offbeats:

```
    -s   +s     +s     +s -s   +s   +s
With scalled browes blake and piled berd.
    o    B   ô B    ô B   o   B  ô B
```

Given a situation with three implied offbeats in the line, it may be easier just to admit that the unaccented *e*'s are pronounced in this instance. If so, the line looks like this:

```
    -s   +s -s   +s  -s  +s   -s   +s -s +s
With scalled browes blake and piled berd.
    o    B o   B o   B   o   B o   B
```

Either way we do it, we save the iambic pentameter structure of the line. The alternate scansions with and without the *e*'s both show the line as structured with very heavy accents. The logic that gives the *e*'s their metrical existence in this heavily stressed line can also give the *e*'s in the following line their existence too:

```
    -s   +s   -s +s -s +s -s   -s   -s +s
An hundred tyme moore than biforn;
    o    B   o  B o   B  o  B̄   o B    (I 3996)
```

Here we have the added complexity of a promoted syllable, promotable only in the context of unstressed syllables. By circular logic, we conclude that the *e*'s must be there or that the line is just defective. The rhythm of the line, however, constructed as it is with its *e*'s and the promotion, gives a definite sense of someone dutifully noting a counting of instances. I wish that I could say that Attridge's system helps in the argument for Chaucer's use of the final *e* in feminine rhymes, but unfortunately all the system does is give us a formula for the feminine ending.

The system, however, does give us a clear sense of how substitutions work into the rhythmic scheme of Chaucer's verse. As noted briefly above, inversions operate as normal rhythmic units of the line and are incorporated in the rules that Attridge uses to describe the abstract pattern of the meter. Inversions at the beginning of the line, for instance, are permissible because of the optional initial offbeat and the optional double offbeat as shown in the abstract form above. This is how the scansion looks (without the stress signs) as applied to a line from Chaucer:

> Milk and broun breed, in which she foond no lak,
> B o   ȯ   B o   B̄ o B   ȯ B   (VII 2844)

In this line, the initial offbeat does not appear, but compensation is provided in the double offbeat following the first beat. In the double offbeat and in the last offbeat, we have a demoted stress, and we also have a promoted stress. This reading clarifies the tension of the line as an iambic line with an inversion, but another reading— certainly more complex in its rendering of the rhythm—is also possible. This reading develops the rhythm according to the heavy linguistic stresses of the line:

> Milk and broun breed, in which she foond no lak,
> B o   B ô B   ȣ   B   ȯ B

We should note the implied offbeat and the triple offbeat that compensate for the heavy stresses of the first half of the line. At first glance, the reading may appear bizarre, but I think that with some pondering and close listening, the reading becomes satisfactory. It incorporates the tension of the line and lets a conversational rhythm develop instead of a more nearly metrical one.

The implied offbeats created by inversions in other places in a line alleviate some of the awkwardness of the shifts in rhythm. The obvious disparity of the stress of the infinitive and the noun in the following line is smoothed by the implied offbeat:

> To han housbondes hardy, wise, and free,
> o B ô B   o   B o B   o   B   (VII 2914)

The implied offbeat allows separation of the different levels of linguistic stress and thus emphasizes the alliteration. Further, there is then no need to pronounce the *e* of *housbondes*. A separation of stresses also occurs in this line with an inversion in what would be the third foot:

> This Absolon knokketh al esily,
> o B o B̄ ô B   ȣ B o B   (I 3764)

The implied offbeat separates the promoted stress of *-on* from the heavier stress of *knok-*, a reading that corresponds to the belief that some linguists have about the pause between subjects and predicates and to the dramatic possibilities of the line. A dramatic reading is also aided by the implied offbeat in this line with an inversion in what would be the fourth foot:

Of studie took he moost cure and moost heede.
o   B o B   o   B ôB   ŏ   B   o   (I 303)

The reading also accommodates the problem of having the same word in the line as both a beat and an offbeat. The first *moost* introduces the superlative qualification and receives stress and a following pause; the second functions almost redundantly, but the tension it provides as a demoted stress gives it rhetorical prominence.

It should be obvious from the discussion of inversions that Attridge's sense of the line as beat and offbeat easily incorporates anapestic movements. Indeed, he accepts a triple offbeat as a possibility, illustrated in an example we discussed above. An anapestic example is given below:

In which she eet ful many a sklendre meel.
o   B   oB o B ŏ   B o B   (VII 2833)

Since strict adherence to a metrical ideal is not important to Attridge, his system has no problems with extra syllables in unstressed positions. Indeed, in the scansions in his book, the offbeats are not marked except when they are in some way unusual or worthy of attention. The overall impression that one gets from reading Attridge is that what is important in English meter is the stresses—the beats. They mark the rhythm and control the force of the line. The offbeat syllables fill in the spaces. That is why the offbeat can be filled with several syllables or no syllable at all. The structure of the line is basically rhythmical; the pulse goes on with or without syllables.

The pulse without a syllable—the implied offbeat—also functions as a justification of the headless line and the line with a "double foot." The optional initial offbeat incorporates both the phenomenon of the initial inversion and the headless line. In music, the first beat begins the measure, and in Attridge's system, the first beat in essence begins the line even in an iambically patterned line. We have seen how the implied and optional offbeat works with inversions; here is how the phenomenon works with headless lines:

Al bismotered with his habergeon,
ôB   o   B o   B̄   o B o   B   (I 76)

Here we have marked the initial implied offbeat, but there is no need to do so, except as a means of signaling that we have indeed noticed the condition. Instances of double feet are somewhat rare in Chaucer, mainly because the final *e* seems to prevent the clashing stress of adjective-noun combinations common in the poetry of Shakespeare. Pairing in the kind of foot scansion we have presented negates the necessity of having double feet, but the following line could qualify as having a double foot. It is scanned first as our system would present it and then as it would be scanned with a double foot:

        x / I x /   Ix / I x / I x /
    For wel he wiste a womman hath no berd. (I 3737)

        x / I x /   Ix / I x x   / /
    For wel he wiste a womman hath no berd.

The double foot serves as a means of illustrating how metrical stress bows to the force of linguistic stress. It is in essence a substitution as justifiable in some sense as an inversion. It is not accepted in the system we have presented here because it denies the process of pairing and weighing of syllables that occurs in foot prosody. However, the scansion has rhythmic justifications.

Attridge's system provides us with the means of accommodating both readings, but the double foot becomes a little unrecognizable because of the implied offbeat. The first scansion given below provides a "straight" reading of the line that accords with the first scansion given above; the second given below takes into account the rhythm of the double foot:

    For wel he wiste a womman hath no berd.
    o B o B o B o B̄ ȯ B

    For wel he wiste a womman hath no berd.
    o B o B o B   ȣ   B ô B

The first reading relies on demotion, to be sure, to allow the alternation of unstress-stress at the line end (*no berd*). Depending on the reader, *hath* may require promotion (as marked) since it is juxtaposed with the quantifier *no*, which has some rhetorical importance. In the second reading, the implied offbeat separates the two stresses and *hath* may be said in some sense to be demoted. The result, in our terms, is a line with an anapestic foot and a metrical caesura—a complication that our system balks at. The acceptance of the second reading, it seems to me, must be based on a rhetorical or dramatical sense of the line. The possibilities here for expression are very interesting.

As we have noted before and as Attridge and other scholars have noted, four-stress meter is different in nature from five-stress meter. A rhythm of four units lends itself well to isochronous tendencies; a rhythm of five units tends to be broken up into groups of twos and threes—an alternation that tends to frustrate isochronism. Since Attridge's scansion tends to emphasize the beat as the important structural unit of the line, his method, with its looseness, eloquently notes the difference between the two kinds of meters. Five-stress meter, even in Attridge's terms, utilizes the offbeats in a more regular fashion than the four-stress meter does. Thus, obviously, four-stress meter depends even more heavily on the beat as the structurally important unit of the line. This is especially notable in Chaucer's four-stress line because of the frequency of headless lines, lines with anapests, and lines with combinations of substitutions— especially headless lines with anapests.

Applying the scansion is an easy matter. Our neutral example from the last chapter is very clear in the application of the scansion:

> And, also domb as any stoon,
> o   B o B   o B o   B   (HF 656)

The implied offbeat that would otherwise fill the gap in these lines presents a metrical argument for the pronunciation of the unaccented *e*'s:

> As burned gold hyt shoon to see;
> o   B o B   o   B   o B

> And soth to tellen, also she
> o   B   o B o   B o   B   (HF 1387-88)

The optional final offbeat, which is preferred in Chaucer's verse, is accommodated in the model <o>BoBoBoB<o>:

> Why this a drem, why that a sweven,
>   o B o B   o B o   B o

> And noght to every man lyche even;
> o   B   o B   o B ȯ   B o   (HF 9-10)

These lines also offer instances of a possible double offbeat (*every*) and of a demotion (*lyche*). The final preferred optional offbeat also accounts for other line-final unaccented *e*'s that do not have syllabic value in Modern English:

> That yt forwot that ys to come,
>   o B o B   o B o B o

> And that hyt warneth alle and some
> o   B   o B o B   o   B o   (HF 45-46)

Once again, the scansion system adds no truly new argument to the problem of whether Chaucer's lines have such feminine rhymes, except in the added circularity of modeling and the fulfillment of expectation from modeling.

Substitutions are handled in the four-stress meter in the same way that they are handled in the five-stress meter. There are initial inversions that drop the optional initial offbeat and compensate with a double offbeat:

> Doun fro the heven gan descende,
> B   ŏ   B o   B   o B   o   (HF 164)

The implied offbeat of inversions elsewhere in the line is illustrated nicely in the following line, in which the implied offbeat occurs at a significant syntactic break:

> And with this word, soth for to seyne,
> o   B   o   B ô B   ŏ   B o   (HF 960)

Double offbeats (anapests) also occur without the implied offbeat condition. Two occur in the following example, which was used in the last chapter:

> Ne in ayr ne in erthe noon element,
> ŏ   B   ŏ   B   ȯ   B o B   (BD 694)

Such an example illustrates well the relative freedom of the four-stress line and its dependence on the beat. The dependence is clearest perhaps in headless lines, where an optional offbeat is left out:

> Whan I first my lady say?
> ô   B o B   o B o B   (BD 1089)

The example we used for presenting the metrical caesura fits well in Attridge's system of the implied offbeat:

> "What los ys that?" quod I thoo;
> o B o   B ô   B o B   (BD 1139)

The combination of substitutions seems less obtrusive in Attridge's scansion. Without foot divisions the headless line with an anapest hardly seems notable, except for the promotion of the first beat:

> By the maner me thoghte so—
> ô B̄ o B   ŏ   B   o B   (BD 453)

If the line still seems light, however, Attridge's system could accommodate the line as a fairly normal three-stress realization of the four-stress line. According to Attridge, and I believe him to be correct, four- and three-stress lines go together well because the three-stress lines have implied beats and offbeats to complete the four-beat rhythm. The syntactic break at the end of this line could fill out the missing measure of rhythm:

> By the maner me thoghte so—
> ŏ   B   ŏ   B   o B o B

In Attridge's system the notion of a line with a combination of a trochee and an anapest is obscured by the all-inclusive notion of the double offbeat:

> Whethir so men wil portreye or peynte,
> B   ŏ   B   ŏ   B   o B   o   (BD 783)

A headless line with a trochee becomes a line with two implied offbeats:

> That was lyk noon of the route;
> ô   B   o   B ô B   ŏ   B o   (BD 819)

Assuming that the double offbeat is a normal part of the rhythm, a line like the one just given is then structurally similar to a line with an initial inversion and a later trochee:

> Ever to be stedfast and trewe,
> ô B   ŏ   B ô B   ŏ   B o   (BD 1227)

   Attridge's system is useful for the sense of the rhythm that it conveys. Although it is not a substitute for foot prosody as a means of understanding the metrical abstraction, Attridge does give us an exciting way of explaining how lines can be or are read. Foot prosody fails in explaining how lines sound; it succeeds as a compositional device that forces the poet into making local judgments with global implications. The results of these judgments are what the rhythmical prosodists attempt to show. In that attempt they are by and large successful. Indeed, they keep us from divorcing the words of poetry from the sounds that can embody them. In a culture given to reading silently, they remind us that poetry is related to music and dance. This duty makes these prosodists valuable to us as literary scholars.

Exercise 7.1

Take the first eighteen lines of *The Canterbury Tales*. Mark the primary stresses in each line. What kinds of patterns do you get? Try reading the lines with appropriate emphasis on these stresses. Is the reading defensibly satisfying? Now try marking the lines to arrive at four-stress line structures. Read this scansion aloud. What processes do you undergo to maintain the four-stress rhythm? What is ignored in this kind of reading? Scan the same lines with Attridge's system as described here. Use this scansion to reconcile the problems you noticed with the four-stress scansion. What does Attridge's system use to fill in the gaps left by the four-stress scansion?

Exercise 7.2

Take twenty lines or so of *The Book of the Duchess* or *The House of Fame*. Mark off the syllables with primary stresses. How many of the lines have four-stresses? How many three? How many fewer? What do you have to do to keep all the lines with either three or four stresses? Scan the lines with Attridge's system as described here. What differences do you see in the handling of unstressed syllables in these lines? Do you see a difference between the way unstressed syllables are handled in these lines and in the lines scanned in Exercise 7.1? Try reading the lines with a heavy musical rhythm. How do they fare? What melodies will fit these lines?

References and Additional Reading

Attridge, Derek. *The Rhythms of English Poetry*. English Language Series, No. 14. New York: Longman, 1982.

Killough, George B. "The Virgule in the Poetry of the *Canterbury Tales*." *DAI* 39 (1979): 5496-A.

Lewis, C. S. "Metre." *Review of English Literature* 1 (1960): 45-50.

Robertson, Stuart. "Old English Verse in Chaucer." *MLN* 43 (1928): 234-36.

Robinson, Ian. *Chaucer's Prosody: A Study of the Middle English Verse Tradition*. Cambridge: Cambridge Univ. Press, 1971.

Southworth, James G. *The Prosody of Chaucer and His Followers: Supplementary Chapters to* Verses of Cadence. 1962; rpt. Westport, Conn.: Greenwood Press, 1978.

—. *Verses of Cadence: An Introduction to the Prosody of Chaucer and His Followers*. Oxford: Basil Blackwell, 1954.

Additional Suggested Reading

A. English Phonology and Versification

Allen, W. S. "On Quantity and Quantitative Verse." In *In Honour of Daniel Jones*. Ed. David Abercrombie, et al. London: Longmans, 1964. 3-15.

Brogan, T. V. F. *English Versification, 1570-1980: A Reference Guide with a Global Appendix*. Baltimore: The Johns Hopkins Univ. Press, 1981.

Brooks, Cleanth, and Robert Penn Warren. "Metrics." In *Understanding Poetry*. 3rd. ed. New York: Holt, Rinehart and Winston, 1960. 119-80.

Cable, Thomas. "Timers, Stressers, and Linguists: Contention and Compromise." *Modern Language Quarterly* 33 (1972): 227-39.

Chatman, Seymour. *A Theory of Meter*. Janua Linguarum, Series Minor, No. 36. The Hague: Mouton, 1965.

—, and Samuel R. Levin, eds. *Essays on the Language of Literature*. Boston: Houghton Mifflin, 1967.

Freeman, Donald C., ed. *Linguistics and Literary Style*. New York: Holt, Rinehart and Winston, 1970.

Fussell, Paul, Jr. *Poetic Meter and Poetic Form*. New York: Random House, 1967.

Gross, Harvey. *Sound and Form in Modern Poetry: A Study of Prosody from Thomas Hardy to Robert Lowell*. Ann Arbor: The Univ. of Michigan Press, 1964.

Guest, Edwin. *A History of English Rhythms*. Ed. Walter W. Skeat. 1882; rpt. New York: Haskell House, 1968.

Halpern, Martin. "On the Two Chief Metrical Modes in English." *PMLA* 77 (1962): 177-86.

Hendren, Joseph W., W. K. Wimsatt, Jr., and Monroe C. Beardsley. "A Word for Rhythm and a Word for Meter." *PMLA* 76 (1961): 300-08.

Kaluza, Max. *A Short History of English Versification from the Earliest Times to the Present Day*. Trans. A. C. Dunstan. New York: Macmillan, 1911.

Lotz, John. "Metric Typology." In *Style in Language*. Ed. Thomas A. Sebeok. New York: John Wiley, 1960. 135-48.

Malof, Joseph. *A Manual of English Meters*. Bloomington: Indiana Univ. Press, 1970.

—. "Meter as Organic Form." *Modern Language Quarterly* 27 (1966): 3-17.

Richards, I. A. "Rhythm and Metre." In *Principles of Literary Criticism*. New York: Harcourt Brace Jovanovich, 1925. 134-46.

Saintsbury, George. *A History of English Prosody from the Twelfth Century to the*

Present Day. New York: Macmillan, 1906.

Shapiro, Karl. *A Bibliography of Modern Prosody.* Baltimore: The Johns Hopkins Press, 1948.

—, and Robert Beum. *A Prosody Handbook.* New York: Harper and Row, 1965.

Stewart, George R., Jr. "A Method Toward the Study of Dipodic Verse." *PMLA* 39 (1924): 979-89.

—. *The Technique of English Verse.* New York: Holt, Rinehart and Winston, 1930.

Waugh, Linda R., and C. H. van Schooneveld, eds. *The Melody of Language.* Baltimore: Univ. Park Press, 1980.

B. Chaucer's Versification and Middle English

Baugh, Albert C., and Thomas Cable. *A History of the English Language.* 3rd ed. Englewood Cliffs: Prentice-Hall, 1978.

Baum, Paull F. *Chaucer's Verse.* Durham, N. C.: Duke Univ. Press, 1961.

Biggins, Dennis. "Chaucer's Metrical Lines: Some Internal Evidence." *Parergon* 17 (1977): 17-24.

Bihl, Josef. *Die Wirkungen des Rhythmus in der Sprache von Chaucer und Gower.* Anglistische Forschungen, No. 50. Heidelberg: Carl Winters, 1916.

Blake, N. F. "Chaucer and the Alliterative Romances." *Chaucer Review* 3 (1969): 163-69.

Bright, James V. "The Rhetoric of Verse in Chaucer." *PMLA* 16 (1901): xl-xlii (Proceedings).

Brusendorff, Aage. "The Canon." In *The Chaucer Tradition.* 1925; rpt. Gloucester, Mass.: Peter Smith, 1965. 43-52.

Burnley, David. "Inflexion in Chaucer's Adjectives." *Neuphilologische Mitteilungen* 83 (1982): 169-77.

Christophersen, Paul. "The Scansion of Two Lines in Chaucer." In *English Studies Presented to R. W. Zandvoort on the Occasion of His Seventieth Birthday.* Amsterdam: Swets and Zeitlinger, 1964. 146-50.

Dean, Christopher. "Chaucer's Use of Function Words with Substantives." *The Canadian Journal of Linguistics* 9 (1964): 67-74.

Deligiorgis, S. "Structuralism and the Study of Poetry: A Parametric Analysis of Chaucer's 'Shipman's Tale' and 'Parlement of Foules.'" *Neuphilologische Mitteilungen* 70 (1969): 297-306.

Evans, Robert O. "Whan that Aprill(e)?" *Notes and Queries* 202 (1957): 234-37.

Everett, Dorothy. "Chaucer's 'Good Ear.'" In *Essays on Middle English Literature.* Ed. Patricia Kean. Oxford: Clarendon Press, 1955. 139-48.

Ferris, Sumner. "A Hissing Stanza in Chaucer's *Prioress's Tale.*" *Neuphilologische Mitteilungen* 80 (1979): 164-68.

Fifield, Merle. *Theoretical Techniques for the Analysis of Variety in Chaucer's Metrical Stress.* Ball State Monograph, No. 23. Publications in English, No. 17. Muncie, Indiana, 1973.

Finnie, W. Bruce. "On Chaucer's Stressed Vowel Phonemes." *Chaucer Review* 9 (1975): 337-41.

Fisiak, Jacek. *A Short Grammar of Middle English: Part One: Graphemics, Phonemics and Morphemics.* London: Oxford Univ. Press, 1968.

Fox, Allan B. "Chaucer's Prosody and the Non-Pentameter Line in John Heywood's Comic Debates." *Language and Style* 10 (1977): 23-41.

Gage, Phyllis C. "Syntax and Poetry in Chaucer's *Prioress's Tale.*" *Neuphilologus* 50 (1966): 252-61.

Gaylord, Alan T. "Chaucer's Dainty 'Dogerel': The 'Elvyssh' Prosody of *Sir Thopas.*" *Studies in the Age of Chaucer* 1 (1979): 83-104.

—. "Scanning the Prosodists: An Essay in Metacriticism." *Chaucer Review* 11 (1976): 22-82.

Green, A. Wigfall. "Chaucer's 'Sir Thopas': Meter, Rhyme, and Contrast." *University of Mississippi Studies in English* 1 (1960): 1-11.

—. "Meter and Rhyme in Chaucer's 'Anelida and Arcite.'" *University of Mississippi Studies in English* 2 (1961): 55-63.

Hammond, Eleanor P. *English Verse Between Chaucer and Surrey.* Durham: Duke Univ. Press, 1927.

—. "The Nine-Syllabled Pentameter Line in Some Post-Chaucerian Manuscripts." *Modern Philology* 23 (1925): 129-52.

Horne, R. H. "Introduction." *The Poems of Geoffrey Chaucer, Modernized.* London: Whittake and Co., 1841. v-cv.

Jambeck, Thomas J. "Characterization and Syntax in the *Miller's Tale.*" *Journal of Narrative Technique* 5 (1975): 73-85.

Joerden, Otto. *Das Verhältnis von Wort-, Satz- und Versakzent in Chaucers Canterbury Tales.* Studien zur Englischen Philologie, No. 55. 1915; rpt. Tübingen: Max Niemeyer, 1973.

Jordan, Richard. *Handbook of Middle English Grammar: Phonology.* Trans. and rev. by Eugene Joseph Crook. Janua Linguarum, Series Practica, No. 218. The Hague: Mouton, 1974.

Knight, Stephen. *rymyng craftily: Meaning in Chaucer's Poetry.* 1973; rpt. Atlantic Highlands, N. J.: Humanities Press, 1976.

Lindner, Felix. "The Alliteration in Chaucer's *Canterbury Tales.*" *Essays on Chaucer, His Words and Works.* Chaucer Society Publications, Series II, No. 16. London: Kegan Paul, Trench, Trübner, 1876; rpt. 1900. 197-226.

Lounsbury, Thomas R. *Studies in Chaucer: His Life and Writings.* 1892; rpt. New York: Russell and Russell, 1962. III, passim.

Lynn, Karen. "Chaucer's Decasyllabic Line: The Myth of the Hundred-Year Hibernation." *Chaucer Review* 13 (1978): 116-27.

Manly, John M. "The Stanza-Forms of *Sir Thopas.*" *Modern Philology* 8 (1910): 141-44.

Masui, Michio. *The Structure of Chaucer's Rhyme Words: An Exploration into the Poetic Language of Chaucer.* Tokyo: Kenkyusha, 1964.

Maynard, Theodore. *The Connection Between the Ballade, Chaucer's Modification of It, Rime Royal, and the Spenserian Stanza.* Diss. Catholic University of America. Menasha, Wisconsin: George Banta, 1934.

Mersand, Joseph. "Chaucer's Romance Rimes." In *Chaucer's Romance Vocabulary.* New York: Comet Press, 1939. 85-89.

Morton, Edward P. "Chaucer's Identical Rhymes." *Modern Language Notes* 18 (1903): 73-74.

Mossé, Fernand. *A Handbook of Middle English.* Trans. James A. Walker. 5th Printing. Baltimore: Johns Hopkins Univ. Press, 1968.

Mustanoja, Tauno F. "Chaucer's Prosody." In Beryl Rowland, ed. *Companion to Chaucer Studies.* Rev. ed. New York: Oxford Univ. Press, 1979. 65-94.

—. "Verbal Rhyming in Chaucer." In Beryl Rowland, ed. *Chaucer and Middle English Studies in Honour of Rossell Hope Robbins*. n. p.: Kent State Univ. Press, 1974.

Owen, Charles A., Jr. "Thy Drasty Rymyng...." *Studies in Philology* 63 (1966): 533-64.

Purcell, J. M. "The 'Troilus Verse.'" *Philological Quarterly* 12 (1933): 90-91.

Pyle, Fitzroy. "Chaucer's Prosody." *Medium Aevum* 42 (1973): 47-56.

—. "A Metrical Point in Chaucer." *Notes and Queries* 170 (1936): 128.

Schlauch, Margaret. "Chaucer's Prose Rhythms." *PMLA* 65 (1950): 568-89.

Smith, Roland M. "Three Notes on the *Knight's Tale*." *Modern Language Notes* 51 (1936): 318-22.

Smyser, H. M. "Chaucer's Use of *Gin* and *Do*." *Speculum* 42 (1967): 68-83.

Stanley, E. G. "Stanza and Ictus: Chaucer's Emphasis in *Troilus and Criseyde*." In Arno Esch, ed. *Chaucer und seine Zeit: Symposion für Walter F. Schirmer*. Tübingen: Max Niemeyer, 1968. 123-48.

—. "The Use of Bob-Lines in *Sir Thopas*." *Neuphilologische Mitteilungen* 73 (1972): 417-26.

Stevens, Martin. "The Royal Stanza in Early English Literature." *PMLA* 94 (1979): 62-76.

Stokes, Myra. "Recurring Rhymes in *Troilus and Criseyde*." *Studia Neophilologica* 52 (1980): 287-97.

Wright, Joseph, and Elizabeth Mary Wright. *An Elementary Middle English Grammar*. London: Oxford Univ. Press, 1923.